Where Dare to Tread

Ruth Farmer

compiled by Irene Hammerquist

ISBN: 9798397282345

DEDICATION

This book is dedicated to my family who supported and encouraged me through the years. Thank you, Dock, for always being supportive. Thank you to my two sons, Gene and John.

I also want to dedicate this book to the many people I have had the honor of serving with throughout the years.

CONTENTS

PREFACE

My mother, Ruth Farmer, got on an airplane for the first time in her life in her mid-40's. Her flight took her to West Africa on a mission trip that began a whole life change as she responded to the call of Christ for her life. She spent most of the next 30 years either in Africa, fundraising in the USA or recruiting people to join with the work that God had set before her.

Ruth was the bravest, most determined person I have ever known. Once when I had helped set up a mission trip for her as she was in her 70's, I met a wonderful and famous preacher in Kenya simply known as 'The Evangelist'. She told me how much she respected and admired my mother and added, "I don't even go where your mom goes. She is an amazing woman of God!" That typified her life and missionary work. My prayer for you is that you will read this and respond to the call of Christ in your life whatever it is with courage and determination.

Pastor John Farmer
(Ruth's Son)

I have always been grateful for the call that God put upon my life. The opportunity to minister alongside so many of the African national pioneer pastors and evangelists in the remote and jungle areas, and to see the hand of God move in the miraculous in their ministries has been awe inspiring. These men have a faith that is unshakable, and this is a good thing, as they minister in such difficult places. They believe in God no matter what they see in the natural, or what the circumstances seem to dictate.

The next best thing to being with them is the testimonies that they send to us. I want to share a few of these testimonies with you in this book. You will be blessed, and in some cases you may be stretched to believe the reports of what God has done to destroy the works of the devil. However, I assure you, that the things that the pastors/evangelists and I are sharing with you took place...they are true. Sometimes truth can be stranger than fiction.

1
CAMEROON, WEST AFRICA

We were finally on our way to Cameroon, and I was excited! It had been many years since Nancy, the mission founder, had been granted a visa to return to Cameroon. The visa had been for all of the missionaries that had been residing in that nation when war broke out twenty years ago, and they had all been expelled.

This is what we were told happened:

For some reason, the officials of the country had decided that some of the missionaries were spies. They issued an order that all missionaries were to be out of the country in twenty-four hours. When this expulsion took place, Nancy had been residing for several years in a remote jungle area for the purpose of taking the Good News of Jesus Christ to the people that lived in the villages that had not yet been reached. Having to leave the relatively new christians created a heartbreaking crisis for her. The new christians would need to have ongoing Bible teaching. Without it, they could quickly return to their old traditional ways, or mix christianity with their former pagan religions. She needed to find a national (or native) that had a working knowledge of the Bible to turn the church over to. And, she had just twenty-four hours to do it. She decided on one of her first converts that lived in a village in the area. After leading him to Christ, she had sent him to Bible School. He was suited for the task. He would assume her responsibility of shepherding the churches that were already planted, continue to evangelize in new areas, and plant more churches as he could. John had done an outstanding job throughout the years. He had kept us informed about the churches that Nancy had planted, as well as updating us about what God was doing as he pushed into new areas. I'm sure angels were singing each time there was a new convert. How exciting it must be for Nancy to now be able to see the converts from so many years ago and to meet the converts that John had led to the Lord. I was excited to finally meet John. I had been doing the foreign mail for Nancy for years, and editing the testimonies that pastors and evangelists sent for the newsletter. I felt as if I knew each one of them on a personal level.

An Arrival Surprise

I had waited for this moment for years…and now we were actually here! I had traveled with Nancy and ministered in other places in Africa prior to this trip. But I never got tired of seeing new places. I enjoyed the thrill of going to African nations that were new to me. However, in spite of my excitement, I had some reservations. First, Nancy hadn't been back here since she was expelled. Secondly, as we walked from the plane to the terminal, I kept thinking of the one issue that could cause a big problem for us. Had evangelist John actually received the letter that I had written to him asking him to meet us at the Douala Airport? No answer to my letter had been received before we left home, but this didn't necessarily mean that he had not written to us. In this particular time frame, mail traveled very slowly to and from Africa. It was even worse when it was to or from a bush area post office. We would not know if he was at the airport to meet us until we had completed the process of checking into the country and arrived at the baggage claim area.

What Now?

Our bags were on the luggage carousel when we arrived to collect them. We then began to walk around the luggage claim area to see if we could find John. But, he was nowhere to be seen. We evidently were on our own since Nancy didn't know anyone in Douala. To make matters worse, she no longer "knew" the city. Twenty years is a long time and surely Douala had changed considerably. With no other options, we headed out to the curb where the taxis were waiting to take on passengers. A taxi driver approached us and asked us where we wanted to go, but there were no markings on his car. We had heard stories of people being taken for "a ride". They were mugged and left in remote areas. In fact, this had happened to one of the ministers that we worked with in Nigeria. He had been robbed, beaten, and left for dead on a jungle road in the middle of the night. God, in his mercy, had sent a vehicle onto this remote road and the driver rescued him. Our decision on whether to take this unmarked taxi was easy, no! After a long wait, we finally decided that we would have to choose a cab and take the chance that it was legitimate. However, even after we were in a taxi, we would still have a problem. Where were we going?

We chose a cab. The driver was getting ready to put the bags into the car when a British man who was standing on the curb and had been in the plane with us, said, "Don't get into that vehicle! You had better come and share my cab, it will be safer." God is so good. We more than relished the idea of not being alone in a taxi, so we thankfully agreed. He asked where we were going and we had to confess that we had no idea. He told us that the hotel where he was going to stay was a really good one. We decided to go with him and to get a room there until we could find a way to get to Mamfe.

Under normal circumstances, we would never have wanted to pay the price to stay at this very expensive establishment, but it seemed the only safe place to be for the time being. We thanked God for the credit card being in hand! The hotel was a quiet place to rest, and that was something we seriously needed. It was always difficult to get our everyday mission work done, ready ourselves for ministry and get everything ready for the trip. Then there were the two days and nights of waiting in airports for flights. Not to mention, the flights to West Africa were very long in and of themselves. We always ended up tired even before we started our schedule. We did nothing except rest and pray for two days. Then we absolutely had to begin to look for transportation to get us to our final destination - Mamfe. This could prove to be a difficult problem to solve. It was a two day trip and Mamfe was in the depths of a jungle. The only bright spot in our situation was that Nancy knew that there was a hotel in this one and only town in this bush location. On the flip side, she didn't know how to find John when we got there. We would at least have a place to stay while she sought a solution to this problem.

Taken For a Ride

On Sunday, Nancy interrupted her rest long enough to attend church. She told me later that she had found the church by asking her taxi driver to take her to a "hallelujah church", so he took her to the only one that he knew about. During the service, Nancy felt that there was something not quite right about the place, but she, not wanting to be judgemental, stayed. (Chalk this one up to learning to listen to that "still small voice" - Holy Spirit) After the service, a man approached her and introduced himself as the associate pastor. They visited for a while and Nancy told him about our need to get transportation to

Mamfe. He told her that he had a vehicle, and that when he had time on his hands, he took people on tours to make extra money. She asked him if he would have time to take us on the two day trip. He said he did and that we could begin the journey the next day. She also told the "associate pastor" that on the way to Mamfe she wanted to buy a used motorcycle to take to John. He said that he had a friend in the town where we would stop for the night who just happened to have a used motorcycle for sale. He would take us to see it.

We arrived at the hotel very late on the first day of the trip. It had been a long drive and we had not eaten. We went to dinner immediately after our arrival and to bed as soon as we got back to the room. The next morning when I woke up, Nancy and the pastor were gone. When they returned for breakfast, Nancy said she had purchased a used motorcycle from one of the pastor's friends. The car that we had driven there in, had been exchanged for a pickup truck that was supposed to carry the motorcycle. However, we started the last leg of the trip without the motorcycle. The excuse the pastor gave for the motorcycle not having arrived was that it was being serviced. It would be coming to Mamfe later in the day. I had never been comfortable with the man, but now my mind was really inquiring! (Holy Spirit) Why had we needed a pickup truck if the motorcycle was not going with us? Why was Nancy not suspicious? She had paid for the motorcycle that we did not have with us. We arrived at the hotel in Mamfe late in the afternoon. We booked our rooms and prayed that John would hear that we were at the hotel. We also asked all of the hotel staff if they knew John, but they did not. There was nothing else to do but to settle in, rest, and prepare to minister after God put everything in place. We had faith that he would work things out. After dinner that evening, Nancy discussed with our minister/pastor escort her need to go to a bank to change travelers checks into Cameroonian francs. He told her that he had a friend that worked at the bank. He could change them for her this evening even though the bank was now closed. He said he had to go back to Douala and he would not be around with the vehicle when the bank opened the next morning. He said that all she would have to do is sign the checks and he would take them to his friend, get the cash and bring it back in about an hour. I personally declined to give him any of my checks. I just couldn't trust this man or his many stories. But, Nancy signed several of her checks and gave them to him. When we went to bed late that night, the man still had not returned, nor had the motorcycle been delivered. He was still not back the next morning. We never saw him again, never saw the motorcycle, and never saw Nancy's money. We had been dumped in the jungle and Nancy had been robbed. Praise God, at least we hadn't been mugged or beaten.

I am ashamed to say that I was on the brink of panic. It took me two whole days to pray the situation through. As the days went by, we continued to ask people that came to eat or stay at the hotel if they knew John. If they did, we asked if they knew where he lived. Finally, we found someone that knew him and where his house was located. Nancy gave the man the money for a taxi to go and get him. It was a huge relief when he finally arrived. I was blessed to meet him. I had been writing to him for so many years that I felt that I knew him personally even though we had never met.

Ministry Begins

In a few days we started to visit the churches that Nancy had personally planted when she had been living in the area. It was a blessing to witness the happiness that she and the older people, the ones she had personally led to Christ, experienced at their reunion. The expressions of joy on their faces was inspiring and made it all worthwhile being there with her. For several days we went from church to church doing ministry. Nancy had the opportunity to again see the converts that she had led to the Lord twenty years prior. After we had ministered in all the closer churches, Nancy and John started to set up the ministry trips to the churches that were located the furthest away. There were two of them. I would be traveling with John to these places since some hiking would have to be done. Nancy would remain behind and minister there. Special transportation would need to be located and arrangements made to get us to the church that was located at the Nigerian border. This would be a very long trip. It would require travel over a very primitive dirt road...and this was the rainy season! It was decided that a taxi driver who used his cab in town would be paid to take John to check out the current condition of the road. However, John unwisely decided to send the man on the mission alone. When the taxi driver came back, he gave the report that the road was passable. (I'm not sure by whose standards, but I wouldn't find that out until later.) John then sent a message to the Otou church leader by a villager that was returning home, that we were coming to minister in their church. As I tell you about the arrangements and precautions that had to be made to prepare for a safe journey, I think you can get an idea as to how much more complicated life can be in remote areas. This was nothing like planning a weekend trip or vacation in America. Every step of the journey required prayer, faith and trust in God. Sometimes God puts us in situations where we must rely on him. He uses these situations to help us grow in our walk with him.

We'll Help - For a Price

John bargained for the price to take us to Otou with a local Moslem man that had a reliable car. He was known to be a man of good reputation. After an agreement had been reached, it was decided that we would be leaving for the Nigerian border in mid afternoon the next day. The driver arrived on time, which is not something that happens often in Africa. We were on our way. We had not traveled very far on this road when a realization hit us. The taxi driver that had been paid to check on the road conditions had not actually done so. As our trip continued to progress, the terrain became more and more steep. The unimproved road was seriously muddy and slippery. My standards of a road in good condition is not the same as road conditions in Africa, or lack thereof. At one point, when our driver was fighting to keep the car on the road, we skidded so close to the edge of the cliff that we could see the floor of the canyon, at least one hundred feet below. The sight that we saw down there must have terrified not only us but also our driver. A truck had skidded off the road and had landed on an outcropping near the canyon bottom.

As our trip progressed, the road became very narrow. There were more and more eroded areas along the cliff's edge. I assumed that the rain was the cause of the erosion, but both John and the driver told me a more harrowing tale. Every year thugs take advantage of the heavy rains and dig away the road's edge on the cliff side. Why? Their purpose for vandalizing the road is financial gain. When the most seriously damaged portion of the road is reached, the drivers that are going to Nigeria must turn off onto a side road that will lead them to a detour that the thugs have constructed. These dishonest opportunists will be found waiting at the detour to charge the drivers to use their crudely set up emergency route. Unfortunately, it was dark by the time we reached the narrow road that led to the expected detour, and the night was very dark. The driver made his way along the road slowly and carefully. When we arrived at the detour, he pulled over to the side of the road and stopped. In a short span of time, the thugs arrived as suspected. They demanded a large sum of money to push us to the top of the hill that they had crudely cleared and called a detour. They were shocked to discover that an American woman was in the vehicle with the two nationals. I'm pretty sure that the price that the driver was quoted for their help went up sharply at that point.

John was overwhelmed and frightened. He was concerned that I might be taken for ransom by these unscrupulous men. He decided that he and the driver would get out of the car and lock me inside while they negotiated a price that could be paid for the men's help. They took John and the driver over to the mountain side and, I assume, talked about the impossibility of the car being able to get to the top of the hill unless they helped by pushing it up. While they were talking, I looked around. The moon was up by this time, and it was a full moon. I could dimly see the sharp slant of the hill. Being married to a man that had been a race driver at one time, I knew some things about cars and what they could and couldn't do. The detour went almost straight up, consisted of slippery mud, and had tree stumps that would need to be avoided. There was no way that these guys could get that car up to the top! The clutch would be destroyed. Unfortunately for John and me, the owner of the car had only driven in civilized settings. And, John had never driven in his life. So to say the least, neither John nor the driver knew or understood the gravity of the situation and what the car was and wasn't capable of. When they came back to the vehicle, I was told that we would be paying these guys to push us up the hill. I voiced my opinion about it not being possible, mentioning that the clutch would likely go out. John didn't want to disappoint the Otou church people…and was terrified for me and my safety.

In Regard to My Well Being

John decided that since all of the thugs would be busy pushing the car, and since he didn't know what could happen to the vehicle during the attempt, he and I would stay behind. We got out and the car was driven to the bottom of the incline. The opportunists got behind it and started to push as the driver pushed the gas pedal to the floor. The engine screamed in protest and the clutch soon started to smoke and burn. In a short time, the inevitable happened, the clutch was destroyed. The car was actually on the other side of the mountain, John and I were not! The vehicle had made it to the top just before it became disabled. It was taken out of gear and rolled to the bottom on the other side.

Jungle, Mud, Mountain Adventure

We were stranded in the jungle with several unscrupulous nationals! (Remember, nationals are ordinary people born and raised in a particular country/area.) Not only were we stranded with them, I was out in the open. In a short time, the car owner hiked back over the hill to get to us. He was fearful for my safety and wanted to get me back in the car and lock me in as fast as possible. This being said, there were two very challenging problems to overcome in order to get me over the hill. The first problem was that the hill was slick with mud, almost a straight up incline, and I was wearing sandals! The second problem was that we had no flashlight. Not only that, the moon had gone behind the clouds. John and the driver could see in the dark better than I could, at least I hoped so. It does seem that the people that live in the dark rural areas in Africa can see at night even when there is little to no light available. My two escorts put me between them and took my hands so they could help me to stay on my feet in the mud. We started up the mountain in the dark. We were slipping and sliding and moving at a very slow pace, but in due time , we arrived at the car.

John locked me inside the vehicle, and prayed double time for a miracle rescue. A few hours went by and no other means of transportation came by. As you can imagine, this road was not heavily traveled in the rainy season for several reasons. But, God is faithful. In due time, God sent an old illegal taxi (no traveling papers) that was coming from Nigeria in the middle of the night. It was absolutely packed with people and cargo. Things were tied on top of and on the outside of the vehicle. It looked impossible for anything or anyone else to fit in or on it. John flagged them down anyway. As it turned out, a woman that attended one of John's churches was inside. Both the vehicle coming along and the church member being inside were "God Things". God had answered John's prayers, or so it seemed. The driver, however, did not want to take on another passenger. He was already overloaded and he would have to stop at the Cameroon border checkpoint. The guard would come out and check the cargo and the amount of passengers. He would also check for traveling documents. The vehicle, being illegal and greatly overloaded, would make bribing him necessary. And, the more blatant the offense, the bigger the bribe would have to be; assuming the guard could be bribed. After a great deal of begging from John and his parishioner, I was allowed to board. I got in with a great degree of difficulty since there was only a sliver of space that the woman next to me could manage. That left me sitting for the most part on what I think was the inside covering for a tire. It was metal and very uncomfortable, but I didn't care. I was on my way to being rescued! It is amazing how God uses situations like this to teach us to have a heart of gratitude. Fortunately for the driver, the mountain coming from the Nigerian side was not very steep and quite manageable even with this load.

High Adventure

It was a great distance to the town and most of it would be through the jungle on a rainy season, muddy road. The Cameroon and Nigerian passengers were not concerned that the journey was a long one. After all, this was "normal" to them. They were busy doing what Africans do; they were singing, snacking, and enjoying each other. As the journey progressed, I began to think about my life. I had been on what appeared to be my death bed when God called me into ministry. If I had heard correctly when God spoke to me about an overseas ministry, I had been given a choice, accept the call or be taken "home". I had decided on ministry. After accepting, God had said, **"I am taking you from a life of just existing, to a life of high adventure."** He definitely had not been joking. This night alone had been adventure packed and a one of a kind experience. I had been stranded in the jungle, surrounded by thugs, and now this - the most exciting part. Here I was, the only Caucasian person traveling through a jungle in Cameroon with the glow of the moon shining on the trees, rescued by an illegal vehicle that was packed with partying Africans. How can life be more adventurous than that!

Check Point

About 1:00 am, we arrived at the Cameroon check point. One of the guards came out to check the cargo that was being taken into the country. It didn't take long for him to find illegal cargo. As it turned out, one of the Nigerians was smuggling electronics. The smuggler was taken inside the guard house, as was a representative for the driver. The driver could not leave the vehicle unattended. The passengers decided to go into the adjacent Mimbo Bar (palm wine - rot gut). Their party would continue in a more well stocked, less cramped venue. One of the ladies invited me to come in with them, but I felt led (Holy Spirit) to decline. I stayed with the driver at the car. A lot of time went by and there was still no sign of the smuggler or the representative. I found that the hardest thing about the long wait was that the moon had again been swallowed up by clouds. The dark was so intense that I don't think I could have seen my hand if I had held it up in front of my face. I had no idea what was going on inside the guardhouse, but it most certainly was lengthy. There were several possibilities for our delay. Perhaps the smuggler didn't have a sufficient amount of cash for a large enough bribe to make the guard happy. Maybe the representative of the driver that went in to negotiate with the official was having problems, lack of traveling papers, short financially, or maybe the guard couldn't be bribed. At last the smuggler was released and the passengers we called back to the vehicle. When the passengers got back to the car, they were even more jolly than they had been when they left for the Mimbo facility. They had not minded the long delay in the least. The singing resumed but twice as loud and their laughter shook the car as the representative said we were free to go.

Hotel Sweet Hotel

We arrived in Mamfe sometime between 3:00 and 4:00 am. The driver tokk us to what seemed to be a central drop off place for passengers. Since he had gone into some serious overtime, he tried to put me out, too. It took a lot more begging by me and by John's church member to get him to decide to take me to the hotel. Finally, we were able to make him realize that a white lady standing on the side of the road in the wee hours of the morning was not a very good idea. God had rescued me again, but not before he had given me what will remain as one of the biggest adventures of my life!

What About Otou

Did we ever make it to the church in Otou? Yes, we finally arrived. Two days later we made our way to the Nigerian border. This time, we went by day, avoided the "killer" short cut, and did not go in our driver, Peter's, car. Peter had to have a mechanic help him get the car. Luckily, the thugs had not stripped it. Nancy and I paid for the mechanic's bill while Peter paid for the clutch. I feel very certain that he never tried to take his vehicle into the bush again, particularly during the rainy season. And, Peter became more knowledgeable about cars - at least what a clutch can and cannot handle. In Otou, I met a group of wonderful christians. We had a really great praise and worship session, as well as the opportunity to minister to the congregation. I also prayed with the "village character". The village character was a drunk according to some of the people that attended the church. It seemed their feeling was that a drunk could not be saved. To these I say: Are you kidding? I have seen a lot of people with alcohol addictions get saved and delivered. As for this "character" being able to be saved, I know first hand.

2
GOD WILL MAKE A WAY

The life of a missionary is never dull. It is always full of surprises, and yes, even shocking circumstances and events. This holds particularly true for missionaries that do pioneer evangelism alongside the national evangelists with which they have partnered. Many of the surprises come in the form of challenges that give God the opportunity to show himself strong and faithful. But there are also delightful surprises that God orchestrates for our encouragement and enjoyment. So let's go back to the start of my life as a missionary.

What's up God
In the beginning of the ministry that the Lord had chosen for me, I had so much to learn! In the midst of a seemingly endless difficulty I began to get frustrated and depressed. I wondered why God didn't seem to be "on the job". I knew in my head that he could do all things, but to me it felt that he was doing nothing to help me. If I couldn't see it, then he wasn't doing anything. This attitude surfaced most often when I was going through prolonged, physically challenging situations that seemed too great to bear. At these times I found myself questioning God. Where are you, Lord? Can't you see I need you? Don't you know I'm near collapsing? I knew that God is the God of the impossible. Yet, the unbearable situation that I was fighting to overcome was still there. God had proven his power over the impossible circumstances in my life long before he called me into ministry. So why this? Why now? In spite of the miraculous things that God had done for me, I still had problems that I had not yet overcome.

I didn't recognize that God was working on my behalf if I couldn't see tangible evidence with my natural eyes. I easily forgot to take into consideration that in most of life's problems, human beings are involved in causing the difficulty. Human beings have a will and God does not override it. We often cause our own delays.

However, in the midst of our weaknesses, God will work to change human minds and hearts. But, it can take time.

11

God Did the Impossible

When God first made it clear to me that foreign missionary work was a job that he had planned for me, I was not "up" to it. I had been fighting for my life for several years. I had been almost totally bedridden for over two years. God touched me and raised me up off of what appeared to be my "death bed". I can't honestly say that all of my physical weaknesses were totally removed. But, my life was saved and I had the strength to answer God's call. Raising me up physically was not the only miracle that God did to get me into the ministry. He also had to convince me that I was actually hearing from him and that he had chosen me to be a missionary. I was forty three years old. His method of convincing me was that of giving me prophecy concerning the call from men and women of God that didn't even know me. I visited many churches when special meetings were being held. In every church I visited to hear a guest speaker, there would be a prophecy that confirmed the call. Since these people didn't know me, I became convinced that I had heard from God. I began to prepare for missions in every way that God showed me to do.

In the proper timing, his timing, God miraculously brought a seasoned missionary into my life, and arranged for me to work with her beginning here in the states. In six months time, I was in Nigeria with Nancy Porter. We would be ministering alongside Nigerian pastors that she had helped train in a Bible School that she had helped build two years before in a remote village there. Our next stop would be Ghana where we would also be doing pioneer ministry work in the depths of jungles in remote areas. Missionary work involved starting new churches to support the walk of new converts, evangelizing and preaching the news of salvation, and bringing the word of God into the remotest areas that had never even heard about God. Couple all of those things with trying to meet their needs and demonstrate God's love through serving others.

God had not only rescued me from the brink of death, he made me capable of doing his work in the hardest of places. I loved the people and the places. Throughout the years, even after Nancy went home to heaven, God would continue to add new places to the West African nations that I was privileged to minister in. In East Africa, Kenya, was part of my life for over twenty-two years. In Ghana, I was blessed to minister alongside a man who was one of the most powerful men of God that I have ever met. I also served in Benin, Togo, Zimbabwe and Uganda. Before you start adding up the years, let me explain. As a missionary/evangelist, you come and go. I lived in Africa about three months total each year, some in West Africa and some in East Africa.

The Bottom Line

All things ARE possible with God; never doubt it! However, remember, it may not be easy. God will make us able if he calls us to do it. God doesn't necessarily call the qualified, he qualifies the called.

Learning to Listen

When God first called me to an overseas ministry, He made it clear that the call was to go into all the world. This was exciting to me. When he revealed to me where I was to begin, it was even more thrilling! I was to begin ministering to Australia and New Guinea.

I started to do all that I knew to do to get myself prepared. I read all of the books that I could find that told me about the Aborigines, a people group I hoped to minister to. It seemed reasonable to me that the Aborigines would be the people group that I would minister to in Australia, since I felt called to the remote and rural places. I could hardly wait until it was time to be about it. (Did you notice all the "I" and "me"s?) I had a lot to learn before the Lord would let me begin. Then, there was another problem. I had no contacts in either Australia or New Guinea. I didn't even have anyone in my scope of acquaintances that had any ties to these nations.

At the Lord's direction, I started doing phone counseling two days a week at a christian television station. When God assigned me this new project, he told me it would open doors for me. It was also great training for ministering to people one on one. Through doing the phone ministry, I met a couple that had been missionaries in Australia and New Guinea for twenty-five years. However, I didn't know this at the time we first became acquainted. The woman called the TV ministry phone line regularly due to some frightening health problems. God used her calls to get us together. Every time she called, she would get my line. Since I had suffered the same life threatening health problems in my past, we bonded. Our friendship progressed to the point that we visited each other's homes. I was delighted when her minister husband told stories of the things that had taken place when he ministered in the Aborigine territory or in New Guinea. He was surprised to find that I felt called to these nations, too. Everything seemed to be falling into place for me to be able to go with them to the mission field when his wife's health returned. But, then everything fell apart. She blamed her mission field years for her illness, and did not want to return. Her husband and I were devastated. Months went by and her condition worsened until she finally died. Worse of all, I had lost a precious friend. But this also closed the door that I was so sure of to minister in Australia and New Guinea. I was overwhelmed on both counts. In regards to ministry, what was I to do now? I had heard God, but had I listened or taken things into my own hands?

Africa! Not For Me

Two years prior to this time, a missionary to Africa had come to speak at the church I was attending. She showed pictures of Africa and told of miracles that God had done as she ministered. I loved her pictures and stories, but I didn't feel anything in my spirit about going to Africa. In fact, truth be told, I didn't want to go. I had seen movies about deep, dark Africa. The continent was literally swarming with dangerous animals. And certain tribes, they were just waiting for a stranger to "drop in for dinner", if you know what I mean. I definitely didn't want any part of it. I would pray for her - but that was it. So when she passed out her bookmarks to remind us to pray for her and her ministry, I took one. I remembered to pray for her for a few weeks, until I lost the bookmark.

A Window Opens
Two years that had passed since the missionary to Africa had been at the church. I had totally forgotten about her, her pictures, her testimony…
Until one day…
Something very strange began to happen in my life. God caused me to start thinking about the missionary to Africa, but I couldn't for the life of me remember her name. She came to mind several times a day. When she did, I saw in the spirit what appeared to be sunshine. It was a happy feeling. I also started having dreams about her. But I still didn't know who she was and I had no inclination in the spirit to try to find her. I thought that she needed prayer and God was reminding me to do that. Several months passed and these things continued to happen.

God's Divine Appointments
I often attended minister's conferences and special meetings at a large church in Phoenix. I lived a long way away from the church and often arrived at the last moment before the meeting began. This meant that I would usually have to sit near the back of the church. This had been the case on this particular day. The sanctuary was literally packed. In fact, I was not only near the back, but I was sandwiched in the middle of a row. When it was time to take a lunch break, the aisles quickly became extremely congested. Those of us that had been sitting in the center of the rows could do nothing except stand and wait for the middle aisle to clear a bit. I was standing and waiting for a chance to exit when I saw a woman that caught my attention. She was in the center aisle. I had no idea who she was, so why had she caught my attention? I had no idea. She was moving with the crowd toward the back door. She was so engulfed by the crowd, that I soon lost sight of her. She did resurface and when she did, you'll never believe where she was. She was pushing her way through the people and making her way into the aisle that I was in. When she reached me she stopped and looked at me and said, "My name is Nancy Porter. Tell me what God is doing in your life." (I finally realized who this lady was - the missionary to Africa.) I answered, "I am mostly thinking about you and praying for you. Do you think God is trying to do something?" She laughed and asked me to go to lunch with her.
We decided that I would come to her house and help her once a week. Little did I know this was how I would begin my journey to the mission field. So

what exactly did I do at her house? The list could go on and on. For starters, I helped to do the filing of letters and reports, did dishes, laundry, and pretty much any household chores that needed to be done. My one day a week soon turned into two days a week…all day. On top of that, other things that needed to be done started coming home with me. I learned a lot in a short time. I got a crash course in missionary's responsibilities, so to speak. I also added conferences and other functions that she asked me to attend with her. In time, I typed up the letters to the pastors and evangelists and edited their reports for the newsletter. I was being readied by God, and by Nancy, for the job at hand. A missionary's life is a life of service. I want you to understand, in spite of Nancy finding me, a woman she didn't know, in a huge crowd, I didn't see that as significant. It still took quite a while for me to realize that the meeting at the conference had been a God thing, a divine appointment.

Within five months, God would have me in a jungle in Nigeria with Nancy with plans to move on to the Ghana jungle. Impossible? Most definitely - yes! I had no supporters. I had never been in an airplane, and I had an absolute terror attack at the thought of flying. This is the short list of "impossible" things that God had to make possible. There were many more impossibilities that God would have to help me overcome…but all these are part of another story. Suffice to say, *God always makes a way even when there seems to be no way. If something is his idea, he will make it happen if we will just cooperate.*

3
CULTURE SHOCK

When I first began the traveling ministry of a missionary evangelist, I had not traveled outside of the USA save a trip to Mexico for medical treatment and a vacation trip to Victoria, BC. Thus, in reality, I had not experienced living in another culture for any length of time. I did have advantages that many people do not have. These helped me cope to a certain degree. I was born in a family of modest means and we lived in a rural area on a farm for several years of my later childhood. This was particularly helpful since I was called to minister alongside pioneer evangelists in rural and remote areas. I think that I would have had a much harder adjustment period had I been raised in an urban setting.

Those of us that have been blessed to live in the USA are, for the most part, spoiled. We have been raised with modern conveniences that we think of as the norm. However, before I go on with this thought, I do wish to recognize the fact that there are great numbers of people in this nation that are living in poverty and do not have these benefits to enjoy. I am writing this to share with you in a fun way, how it was for me when I first started in ministry. Remember this was before the time of the internet and easy access to pictures and information from other countries and cultures. Keep in mind this fact, I LOVE AFRICA AND THE AFRICAN PEOPLE. I am absolutely blessed beyond words by the ministry that God called me to do!

Consistently Foreign

It didn't take me long to learn that no matter which African country God sent me to, things were going to be vastly different. There was no point in analyzing the way things were being done or not being done. My mind simply could not grasp the African mind set and thinking. In turn, they could not reason as I reasoned. They didn't understand that their way of doing things was unusual in my way of thinking. Simply said, they do not think like we think nor do we think like them. This is to be expected, of course, since our realms of experience have been vastly different. We must remember when we are in another nation, that we are the foreigners. Patience, a good sense of humor, and an adventurous spirit are valuable tools that will enable us to succeed when we are faced with a situation that produces culture shock. These attributes are important if we are to consistently be a light that shines for Christ. These virtues will also enable us to make lasting friendships. So let me explain some of the differences that impacted me as I tried to learn the flow of things in this new country.

African Time

My first major lesson to be learned was that of African time. The pastor of the church that we were speaking at would tell us what time the service was to begin. I noticed that each time he did so Nancy, with a smile, would ask him, "Is that actual time or African time?" The pastor always laughed and said, "The people will begin to arrive about..." and he would give an estimated time when we would most likely see them. This could be, and usually would be, from one to two hours late.

During my first trip to Nigeria and Ghana I began to understand that there were three reasons for this faithful lateness. The first reason is that almost everyone has to rely on public transportation. Then there are many people that can't afford public transport and must walk. They walk together in groups and chat as they go, kind of like a social gathering. The second reason for African timing is that the Africans are not uptight. They take life as it comes with a happy heart. Their attitude: I'm going to be late. Oh well, not much I can do about it. -OR- They will get here when they get here. Let's just visit. After many times of watching Nancy make the most of her time as we were waiting for the pastors to pick us up, I saw that she had adopted this same attitude. She had learned to wait patiently during her multitude of years living in the jungles of several African nations. As the years passed, I became better at waiting. I stopped wasting so much time fretting. It was a lesson that was hard to learn. The third reason that may have contributed to the villagers' lateness is that they do not have watches. A great number of the people lack timepieces of any kind. However, I am quite sure that even if they did have watches, the first two reasons would prevent them from being punctual.

I would like to note that their tardiness is not out of disrespect in any way. Once people got there, whether early or late, it was like a social event. They weren't in a rush to leave. They never complained if the missionaries were late. They would just visit with others and enjoy seeing one another. Like I said, they take life in stride, happily and stress free. These times were special to them and brought much joy.

Transportation Woes

The nature of our ministries involved traveling overland for very long distances almost daily. This meant that everyday we experienced either the problems of trying to find public transport, or the mechanical failures of the well worn cars that had been arranged for us by our pastor friends. These cars may or may not have been aged. It does not take long for a vehicle to become decrepit when it is used on rural and jungle roads. The condition of the roads, both dirt and tarmac, were to say the least not good. And that is putting it mildly. These roads could make American dirt roads look like freeways. In fact, roads were virtually nonexistent in many places where the men we ministered alongside had ministries. Whatever the cause of a vehicles mechanical failure, the result was that a trip that was estimated to take six or seven hours would usually take ten or eleven hours. There were a great variety of reasons for our transportation failing us. Many of them were quite dangerous. At these moments, it was easy to understand why the phrase WAWA had come into existence. WAWA was a term that missionaries who worked in West Africa for a long time had come up with. This term was used in difficult situations when they had lost a "battle" and a situation had won. However, when they said it, they were laughing. WAWA means: West Africa wins again! I want to clarify here that the same missionaries that coined this term would not have wanted to quit working in West Africa. We all loved the people and what God has called us to do. When I think back on the difficulties, particularly on the roads, situations that were hard to solve, or dangerous circumstances, I smile. Many of these recollections are now precious memories. God showed himself strong on our behalf to rescue us from many of them. The problem often produced adventures that I would not have wanted to miss. I will share more of these accounts later.

A Good Report

No matter what time of night we arrived at the church or our venue, the congregation and the pastor in charge would still be there singing and praising God. God's Spirit was in their midst. He does inhabit the praises of his people! And last but not least,we always arrived safely, no matter how dangerous the cause of the delay had been.

Purpose of the Gas Can

We spent very little time in a town or city. When in a metropolitan area, it was usually necessary to use a taxi. The memories that really stick in my mind concerning taxis and taxi drivers are funny now. At the time, the absurdity of the situations that we encountered were not humorous at all. I will repeat myself here by saying that I cannot think like an African, nor can they think like I think. A good example is the way I view the intended use of a gas can in regards to a vehicle. I was raised to believe that a gas can should contain fuel at all times to be used in case of an emergency. But, judging from my experiences with the national taxi drivers, their view is totally different. Judging from what I've seen, the gas can, in their way of thinking, is to take to get gas **after** the tank is empty. This empty tank also happened at the most inopportune times. It seemed to happen more often than not on a rural "shortcut" that had been taken to save time on the way to the airport to take the foreign visitor to catch a plane. One particular situation that I will never forget, was being stranded on a very desolate road at night. The reason being, you guessed it, an empty gas tank and an empty gas can.

Shortcut, Patience and Prayers

The shortcut the driver chose on this particular night was not new to me. Numerous taxi drivers had taken us on it throughout the years. The familiarity with the road made me feel apprehensive from the moment we turned on to it. This was a road that was very rarely used, especially at night. It was definitely no place to have an emergency, but the unthinkable has a way of happening. After we had gone several miles, the car's engine started to sputter. The driver pulled the vehicle off the road into the weeds and got out to check the situation - as if that was necessary. After a very few minutes, he pulled his head out from under the hood and announced, "We are out of petrol." I could have easily predicted what he would say next, which was that the gas can was empty, too. He took the can in hand and stood by the road. At least he tried to appear hopeful that another vehicle would come along soon and he could get a ride back to civilization to get gas. (Mind you, I had been on this stretch of road before.) Even more frustrating was that we could see the lights of the airport. In reality, it was two to three miles away. This sounds like a doable walk. Right? Remember, I was in Africa, in a remote area, and not on the paved streets of the good ole USA. We also had a large load of luggage consisting of two suitcases each and hand luggage, making it impossible for us to manage. Not to mention, the time of our flight was quickly approaching. Thoughts of having to watch our plane leave without us filled our minds.

NOTE: I would like to take a quick moment to explain something I've learned over the years. When God has a job for you to do, he provides you with an anointing to do that job. When God would send us on mission trips, there was an anointing upon us and we were filled with joy to go and see all God would accomplish. We were excited, even in the trials, because we were filled with the Holy Spirit. But, when the job is done and the anointing lifts, the desire to get home becomes first and foremost in our thoughts and minds. In other words, we love to go when God is sending us. But when we know in our spirit that our job is done, it is hard to think about anything except getting home and seeing families. This was our mindset at this point in time.

We prayed. We prayed hard and fervently for the miracle of another vehicle to come by on this desolate stretch of road in the late hours of the night. We prayed that a driver would come that had gas in their gas can or a driver that would take our driver to fill his empty gas can. And wouldn't you know, God is faithful and merciful! He heard our prayers and in due time he rescued us. A car did come by and the driver stopped to see if we needed help. The man took our driver to get gas. In African time, they arrived back. God often moves in the eleventh hour. We got to the airport in a nick of time. We did a last minute check in, praying all the while that our luggage would make it on the same plane as us. We had to get to Lagos and make our connecting flight to Amsterdam and then a third flight home to the USA. The bags did all arrive with us and we arrived home on schedule. We had survived another situation that tested our patience. And, we got to see the hand of God rescue us once again.

Reflecting back, I realize that the trials of life that we must pass through will draw us into a deeper faith in God, ***if we don't crumble in the process.***

4
BACK UP: MY FIRST MISSION

Let's back up to get a glimpse of how it all began. Yes, I was definitely excited to have been called by God to be a missionary. But there were many things I didn't know. There were even more things that I needed to learn. When God sets you on a new path, you need to have a teachable spirit. There is no room for arrogant know-it-alls.

And so it began

Our plane had landed two nights ago in the huge city of Lagos, Nigeria. Since that time, we had been trying to get some rest before starting our two month long mission. This was my first mission, and in fact as I mentioned earlier, it was also my first time to travel any further from the US than Mexico or Victoria, B.C. I can tell you that what I was feeling was a conglomeration of excitement, fear, joy, and expectation mixed with a hefty sprinkling of awe. You can be sure that what I had seen so far of Nigeria was nothing like anything I had seen up until this time. When he initially called me to foreign ministry, God had told me that he was taking me from a life of merely just existing to a life of high adventure. I had thought that perhaps I had not heard him clearly. But, I was beginning to suspect that I had heard him quite accurately. Being an adventurer at heart would most likely be in my favor.

Hotel rating?

The hotel that Nancy's pastor acquaintance had secured for us had been booked with an eye on our finances, not necessarily our comfort. This was good, but this particular establishment was definitely not a five star hotel. In fact, it was not even a half star rated facility. However, as we would soon learn, it was not without its own merit. It had one real plus. The staff members desired to serve us well. The only problem we were having with them was that they were extremely nervous about having Caucasians in their hotel. It was obvious that this was a new experience for them. We did our best to encourage them and put their minds at ease.

Scouting for rooms

Our initial challenge on the first night was to find rooms that actually had amenities or rather to be more accurate - necessities, or at least as many as possible. A working air conditioner was a top priority. The next thing to watch out for, according to Nancy, was to check the bed. She said to be sure it was something you could live with… and hopefully sleep in. The last two important things were to determine if the lights worked and do a sniff test for mold. We were both allergic to it. Nancy informed me that mold could be a problem throughout our trip since Nigeria has so much rain and therefore high humidity. Mold seemed to be no problem in this room that we were currently being shown. It did have one serious shortcoming. The light bulb that was dangling from the ceiling - like those you see in an interrogation room on movies - was burned out. At least that is what we thought since it wasn't working. We asked if another bulb could be brought to replace it. We were told that the electrician would not be in until the next day. We assumed that since you don't need an electrician to replace a light bulb, that there must be a specific person assigned to handle all electrical problems.

You are probably wondering if we checked the bathroom to see if everything there worked. Yes, we had. But I became disheartened when I learned that the toilet would not be flushable. We were told that the reason for this problem was that the water in the city of Lagos was turned off most of the time. Nancy told me later that either the city or the hotel staff could be responsible for the turn offs. She had experienced this problem for many years and wasn't concerned. "You just make the most of every drop of water." She explained that we must make sure that we were each issued a water bucket before the staff members left us for the night. Then every morning, very early, we would send for a porter to take our bucket and fill it. That bucket of water would have to last us all day and all night! It had to be enough for baths, hair washing, laundry, and toilet flushing… the later being the last use for the water, of course. The water from bath, hair, and laundry was recycled for the once a day toilet flush that this amount of water could provide. The rest of the day, we would need to put flushing on hold. Water management was just the beginning of the many things I would have to learn to survive, and to do it well, as we would be continuing to minister throughout the nation in the years to come.

The biggest lesson of all that I had to learn, and to remember was this. No matter what nation we were in, "It was not going to be like America!" The differences were always going to be substantial, to say the least!

The first morning

Our first morning in the hotel started very early, much earlier than I had anticipated. At about 5:30 AM, the stewards started doing their daily chores. Being an exuberant group, the clanging of buckets, shouts to each other, and laughter filled not only the halls but also our rooms. An important reason for this early start was that the water was flowing at this hour of the day. That made getting many of the chores done in this time frame absolutely essential since water was required to do them.

Nancy and I both realized that pillows over our heads didn't drown out the noise. Being unable to sleep, we dressed and went down for breakfast. The waiter escorted us to a table and went to the kitchen to see the cook. The cook came out to see us and seemed to be blown away that he was going to be cooking for white people. He asked us what we normally eat for breakfast. He seemed greatly relieved, breathing a sigh, when we told him that an omelet and toast would be fine. A lot of time passed before the omelets were brought to us. Nancy said that she was pretty sure that the waiter had to go to the market for the eggs. Hotels that cater to the Africans usually do not have refrigerators. In due time, our breakfast was served. This was my first encounter with an African style omelet. It sat on the plate swimming in palm oil. I am assuming that this is the way people in that nation like it. Nancy, being seasoned in African ways, ate her omelet, palm oil and all. I decided to pull my eggs out of the palm oil and I found out that the omelet was quite good. We sent for the cook after breakfast so we could tell him that he had done a great job. He beamed and bowed, and thanked us profusely. He was just as eager to please us as the stewards were.

Unlikely entrance

Nancy had arranged with her minister friend who pastors a church of five thousand people to allow us to teach at a women's conference. The conference was to take place on the third day that we were to be in Lagos. He said he would send a car to pick us up and take us to the venue. On the day of the conference, we readied ourselves for the meeting and sat down to study our material/notes. We waited and waited for the car, but it never came for us. The hotel had no phone and in all likelihood, the church we were going to probably did not have a phone. I was to learn throughout my years of ministry that there was rarely any phone service in West Africa, even in the cities. This is particularly true in Nigeria, unless it had perhaps been available in high end hotels. This most definitely and consistently left us out!

We had no idea why the car was not coming. Perhaps the pastor had forgotten to send it, or maybe it had broken down. This hotel was in a rural area, consequently there was no traffic passing by and no newcomers had arrived at the hotel on this particular morning. We were stranded and the hour of the conference was fast approaching. We needed a plan. Nancy, being experienced in such things, went outside and stood in front of the hotel to see if she could find any kind of transportation. In time, she did find a ride for us. And, "any kind of ride" is exactly what she found.! After some time, a beer truck arrived to make a delivery. She approached the driver and told him about our problem. After much protesting on his part, he and his assistant agreed to crowd together in one of the bucket seats and allow us to share the other seat. They would take us to the church. Nancy, being great at witnessing, took advantage of every moment that it took to reach the church. She told the two men about Jesus and his love for them. She testified about how she had received Christ. I don't know the outcome of her efforts, but they had heard the good news. A seed had been planted. And isn't it God who causes it to grow anyway?

As you can imagine, the beer truck pulling into the church parking area attracted a lot of attention! There was no shortage of onlookers. The gawking group consisted of a few hundred women, and perhaps a pastor or two. The awkward stares didn't concern Nancy. She had learned over the years of her ministry to take everything in stride. She had likely experienced many unusual situations during the years of ministering to people in the African bush. She came down out of the truck with as much poise and dignity as a queen, and I followed with as much as I could muster up at that moment. We alighted just as if a beer truck was the appropriate conveyance in which to arrive at a church.

The women's conference

The conference was to take place in a large windowless building. The lighting, though electric powered, proved to be dim at best. We were doubtful that the ladies would be able to see the print in their bibles sufficiently enough to follow along with Nancy as she read the scriptures. Of course, this would not be a problem for a large percentage of the women. They were by and large from rural villages. Most did not own a bible and many of them had never had the opportunity to learn to read.

NOTE: School is not free to the students in most African nations. The parents must pay and the cost can be far above the financial possibility of many, especially since so many kids must go to a boarding school. This is due to their remote area home locations and because of the lack of transportation near their villages. Another reason some do not have the opportunity to go to school is because they must help care for the family's garden plots or be responsible for other jobs in their family.

Conference time

By now it was almost time to start the conference. The building was filled with ladies, in fact, the occupants had pushed together to the extreme. In America, it would be against the fire code and we would feel squished and need our own space. I was to learn in my ministry that there is a saying in most African nations. *"There is always room for one more."* These people graciously try to accommodate others in crowded spaces, including transportation vehicles as well as buildings.

The praise and worship time was awesome! These women knew how to put their all into praising God. It was like an open heaven and I loved it! After praise, Nancy ministered the word and the women listened intently. Nancy was not new to many of them. She had been a friend of the pastor for many years, and as such, had ministered at various times in this church. Her message concentrated on believing that God can do all things. In short, have faith in God for what you need from him. Nancy was still teaching when a loud clap of thunder seemed to almost shake the building. The electricity failed immediately, thrusting us into total darkness and leaving us without a PA system. Immediately, the natural heavens opened and a cloud burst started a torrential downpour. At this point we learned something about our venue that we hadn't noticed, it had a tin roof. You have not heard rain until you have been in a tin roofed building during a downpour! Nancy tried to stall with finishing her message. The building was large and her natural voice would not only not be heard in the back, but most likely not even in the front rows. The rain continued to beat on the roof. She finally gave up and told the women we would pray for them and their needs individually. The prayer line formed and we started praying. The women had to scream their prayer request into our ears so as to be heard. Then we winged it with our prayer, as we were not sure we had heard correctly. We shouted as we prayed, hoping the lady we were praying for could hear our prayer and be encouraged. The rain was still coming down relentlessly when we finished praying for those who needed or wanted prayer.

The rest of the story...
In this first ministry time of my mission experience, I got an inkling that a missionary must find a way to do their job even in the face of seemingly impossible situations. The second thing, a very important lesson to learn, we may not always know what takes place in the hearts of the people when we minister. I have no idea what the impact was as a result of our ministry to the women that day. There were no testimonies, there couldn't be. And by the end of praying, we had all strained our throats to the breaking point. The rain was still pouring when we finished and dismissed everyone. I left feeling unfulfilled. Throughout the years I have learned that it is not about me. My job is to do what God sent me to do and have faith in him to do the rest. The outcome is his responsibility and he is a faithful God!

5
ORDINARY TO DO EXTRAORDINARY

Sometimes you feel like just an ordinary person. You don't feel worthy of doing great things. But our God uses ordinary people to do amazing things. He calls the unqualified and he qualifies them to do his will. This requires faith and trust in him. I think that is why he does it that way.

Enugu, Nigeria
The flight from Lagos to Enugu was eneventful. I spent the whole time looking out the window and appreciating the Nigerian terrain. The flight's altitude was low enough that I could see an amazing amount of the countryside. This was a blessing since we had flown into Lagos at night. All I had seen of Africa, until this time, had been the portion of the city and rural area that we had driven through on our way to the hotel and the venue. The flight time passed so quickly for me that I was surprised when the announcement came that we were preparing for the plane's landing.
As we descended the steps of the plane, I heaved a sigh of relief. The heavy spiritually oppressive atmosphere of the big city was not present here in Enugu. In Lagos, I had felt almost overwhelmed because of the tremendous spiritual oppression. I suppose that my awareness of the spiritual climate was due to the fact that I had never been in a city that had such a large occult presence, and it was my first time in Africa. Now that I was in Enugu, which was a much smaller city, it felt to me as if a heavy load had been lifted off me.

Walking and thinking
There was no gate available for our plane, so the plane had to be parked quite a long distance from the terminal. There was also no bus, so we would need to walk the remaining distance to the terminal. The long walk would be no easy task for me since my hand luggage and my travel purse were quite heavy. In West Africa, hand luggage and purses were not weighed by the national airlines and these bags traveled free. I thanked God for free travel for hand luggage since we had in-country flights and a flight from Nigeria to Ghana. These two bags could easily have weighed thirty-five pounds. Necessity was

my reason for carrying this heavy load. This was my first mission and I had no ministry supporters to help me financially. Add to that the numerous expenses to be covered in addition to my air travel. The extras included housing, food and overland travel (We would be traveling a huge amount of miles daily after we left the Bible School that was located in a small village in the heart of the jungle. We would then be ministering in the churches that had been planted in remote areas by the pastors that Nancy had helped train for ministry.) During this mission, we would also be going to be with the pastors that had been assigned to the Moslem territory in northern Nigeria. We would minister in their churches, and hopefully they would be encouraged. None of the assignments that her former students had been given were easy, but they had all been raised in jungle settings; this would help. In addition to the above mentioned things, I was also expected to share the expenses for our ministry outreaches, and to help the national pastors financially with their everyday costs. These expenditures would be ongoing for the eight weeks of our mission in both Nigeria and Ghana.

To help strengthen my faith concerning finances, I dwelt on the fact that God had paid my way thus far. But my mind still kept asking the question, "Are there sufficient funds for the extras?" I didn't know the answer to this question in the natural realm, but I did know that God had sent me, and he doesn't send us out to be defeated.

As I mentioned, the purpose of our stay was to connect with Nancy's pastor friend, "the Apostle". He was called "the Apostle" by all of the pastors that he was in charge of overseeing as well as by their congregations. We would be visiting many of their churches and would have the joy of ministering alongside them. Sometimes it would be in areas where they wanted to get a new church started. While we awaited his arrival, I had many unusual experiences and opportunities. I was also feeling a great deal of sadness because I had to leave my husband at home. We had not been apart for very long during our then twenty-eight years of marriage. To make matters worse, there was no way for us to communicate. Technology was not available like it is today and mail was not an option. Even if I mailed him a note, it would take months to make it to the United States. If he mailed me a note, we would be traveling and didn't have a consistent location. There are many things that weigh on your mind as a new missionary.

Luggage limits

We were allowed to check in two bags, but they could only weigh forty kilos each. This isn't much when everything that we could possibly need for the eight weeks had to be with us. Packing took a lot of planning because if you didn't pack carefully, it could cost you dearly. Any weight over the allowed limit was charged an extra fee per kilo, and it was not a small sum. Although the weight sounds like a sufficient amount, you must consider the jungle rule of thumb. "If you want it, you had better arrive with it!" There was often no time to shop and very few places to shop.

There were things you had to pack when going on a mission that the typical American traveler would never even think about. This list included but was not limited to: a sheet, small pillow, towel, soap, water pitcher, drinking glass, plastic plate, silverware, emergency snacks for when there was no food available, mosquito repellent, medication, first aid kit, laundry detergent, thin rope, flashlight/batteries, matches, toilet paper, and duct tape. Duct tape, as I would come to find out, serves a multitude of purposes. It can be used to cover a window in the bathroom when the common area is right outside that window, mend almost anything, hold a broken shoe together, cover a wound, the list goes on. Likewise, rope served many purposes like tying shut a door that has no lock, or securing your luggage closed after the zipper breaks during the security check at the airport when we were to board a flight to another country. (Yes, these things did happen during my years ministering in Africa.)

Negative and positive

The negative emotions that I was experiencing stemmed from fear. But, they did not crowd out the excitement that I was feeling about the adventures that lay before me. Adventure is the word the Lord gave me. That's what he was calling me to. To be exact, he had said, "I'm calling you from a life of existence into a life of high adventure and productivity." Considering the fact that I had been near death for sometime before God called me, adventure sounded great to me!

The ministry begins

We made our way through all the checkpoints without delay and were blessed to find Nancy's pastor friend, Rev. Godwin Ekpe there to meet us. He had made reservations for us at a hotel. I was excited, it had 'palace' in its name. He said the nationals liked to stay there because the rates were reasonable and their restaurant served good food, both African and European. The hotel was okay, but it most certainly did not live up to its name. The word 'palace' conjures up visions of splendid surroundings. Although it fell short of splendid, it was adequate. It was adequate with the exception of one thing we were soon to find out. As soon as the sun set, we realized our room was directly across from and one floor above the disco. Our first night in this 'palace' was a Saturday night. The sound of blaring music and revelry lasted most of the night. It was a night I will never forget!

I eventually fell asleep in spite of the loud music and partying. However, I did not stay asleep. I awoke sometime between one and two in the morning and realized that my spirit was very disquieted. I opened my eyes and was shocked to see 'things' (demonic spirits) coming out of the walls. The first thing that came to mind was, "Is God revealing them to me or are they manifesting?" I wasn't sure at first, but I believed they were manifesting. As strange as it may sound, it appeared that they were dancing to the music! After the initial shock of what I was seeing had worn off, I remembered being taught that in Jesus' name I had authority over demonic spirits. So I spoke to them in his name, telling them to get out of the room. Nothing appeared to change, they were still in my room. So, I spoke a second time and they became aggressive and rushed over to my bed, shaking it violently from side to side. I held on to both sides of the bed as tightly as I could so I wouldn't fall off. I again told them, "Get out of this room in Jesus' name. They then appeared to rush out of the room right through the walls or back into them.

Nancy always slept with ear plugs (I need to add those to my list of things to pack.) so she slept soundly all night. I told her about the experience the next morning. Her comment about the bed shaking was nonchalant, "Oh, they do that all the time. The bed shaking was to try to intimidate you." Of course, she had not mentioned to me, a new missionary, that these kinds of things go on in African hotels. She explained that the hotel rooms are often inhabited by demons because of the great sexual sin and demonic practices that go on in them. As the mission progressed, I learned that she was right. These things happen quite frequently. Weeks later when we were in Ghana, I mentioned my experience to Pastor Victor. His response, "Oh, they do things like that all the time." Apparently, these things also happen to nationals.

Another shortfall

The hotel was packed, so changing rooms was not an option. This room was ours for the duration of the stay. The hotel was hosting a large gathering of chiefs and tribal leaders that ruled over various areas of the country. They were having a convention there for a week. Since they were Moslem, the rising of the sun revealed yet another shortfall for the location of our room. Next to the disco in the small courtyard, just below our window, is where the chiefs and leaders did their praying. Morning prayer was at dawn. The sound of their prayer chants was defeaning. As you may know, these prayers are repeated several times a day. Peace and quiet for any length of time would be out of the question for us.

Lay over days

As mentioned earlier, we were to be in Enugu for a few days. The day we would leave depended on when Pastor Godwin, or the Apostle, came back to pick us up and take us to the Bible School that he and Nancy had established several years before in the jungle area. We would be ministering at the school for a couple of weeks and at the church that he had planted on the same property. Then we would be visiting as many of the 50 ministers that Nancy had helped train as possible. After their graduation, many had been assigned to pastor churches that for the most part were scattered across the country. Others had planted churches in jungle areas, and some had been sent to do evangelism in the Moslem North. Nancy was excited to get to see some of her former students and be able to minister in their churches.

In the meantime, Pastor Ekpe and his wife, Comfort, would be showing us around and setting up ministry opportunities for us during our stay in Enugu. They were a blessing and I greatly enjoyed being with them and hearing about their ministry.

"Thrown" into foreign ministry

The most exciting thing for me that took place during our layover was that I had my first opportunity to teach God's word in a church service in Africa. The opportunity came as a surprise. God has a sense of humor and pushes us out of our comfort zone into the things he has called us to. Comfort was a nurse at a small clinic on the edge of the jungle. Pastor Ekpe sometimes ministered in the evenings in that facility. He had what he called a very effective outreach method that he also used in jungle villages. On our second night in Enugu, Pastor Ekpe planned such an outreach at the clinic. We had dinner, loaded up the car, and we were off to our first ministry of the trip. About an hour before start time, Pastor Ekpe put his effective outreach plan into motion. Phase one, the loud speaker was put to good use. He turned it up as loud as it could go and announced that there would be a free movie being shown at the clinic. He turned it up and shouted so as many villagers as possible in the distant villages could hear about the movie. The hope was that the sound would carry throughout the entire town and beyond to the fringe of the bush. The response was quite good. By the time the movie was ready to begin, between sixty to seventy-five people had come in and sat down to wait. Phase two involved a generator, a film projector, a christian movie and a huge bed sheet to project the movie onto. The movie subject for this evening was the rapture and the people that had been left behind. The people in the audience were "enraptured" by the movie. They were watching it intently when to everyone's surprise, including ours, Ekpe stopped the film at the midway point and had an intermission. The audience was NOT happy about the interruption. Pastor Ekpe assured them that it would resume and the end of the film would be played after the message. He asked them not to leave. He then asked Nancy to come and minister to the people, but she did not feel up to it. Then out of the blue she asked me to speak to the people. I was almost in shock! I had not prepared anything to present (I like being well prepared.). What would I preach? God needed to lead me because I certainly didn't want to turn down this opportunity that I had been thrown into. After all, that is why God had sent me, right? I prayed and then pulled a book of God's promises out of my purse and opened it to the subject of God's love. I did all that a person in this situation could do. I allowed the Holy Spirit to draw my eyes to specific scriptures and fill my mouth with what I believed was his thoughts on those scriptures. God is so faithful! The whole thing flowed smoothly. At the end when I gave the opportunity for the people to receive Jesus, about fifty of the listeners came forward. This was an awesome testimony to me on the faithfulness of God. When we can't - GOD CAN! Pastor Ekpe then turned the movie back on as promised. I'm not positive, but an uprising might have occurred if he hadn't.

Just saying…

God uses ordinary people to do extraordinary things! All that needs from us is a heart that is willing to trust him, and our willingness to step out in faith as he leads. If we are not willing to be thrown or pushed out of our comfort zone, there is a remedy. We must simply have an attitude that says, "Lord, I am willing to be made willing." It can at times be an almost heart stopping experience to step out in faith. But is stepping out in obedience to God… especially when we know for sure that we are not equal to the task. That's why it is extraordinary. And, it will become easier if we remember that it is God's ability that will accomplish the job and not our own.

And you…

The Lord has some surprising and exciting things that he wants to accomplish through you. My advice is to let go and let God use you. You will be glad you did! I was so happy that I didn't let fear stop me.

1 Thessalonians 5:24 KJ
Faithful is he that calleth you, who also will do it.

Philippians 4:13 KJ
I can do all things through Christ which strengthens me.

6
ISIOBO-NARA BIBLE SCHOOL

At last, the day for our trip to the jungle arrived. We got up early to make the needed preparations for the journey to the bible school which was located in the jungle village of Isiobo- Nara. The car was loaded with our luggage and the necessary supplies. We were on our way, my excitement mounting. The tarmac road could be taken for a relatively short time before we had to turn off onto the unimproved road that led to the interior. This road was heavily rutted and covered with potholes. The driver carefully maneuvered around the largest holes.This slowed us down to a snail's pace, but I didn't mind. I was so caught up in the beauty of the jungle that I hardly noticed. When we finally arrived at the school, the cook excitedly ran out to the car to greet us. She then turned to me and proudly told me that I would be staying in her room. She would move to the pantry room next to where I would be. She then gathered up all my bags and led me to my quarters. After she had shown me around the place, she anxiously asked me if I could manage it. I told her that I would be fine. I did, however, ask if she could get me a small fan. The extreme heat affected me so much physically. She said that it might be possible and went off to check with a friend.

Jungle lessons
During our stay at the bible school, I learned many things from my friend, Chenurea the cook. The times that we both had a few minutes to spare, we took walks. She taught me about jungle life as only a national would be able to do. I am so grateful for these experiences. I also learned a great deal by my everyday observations. One thing that stood out to me was that the living conditions that I experienced in rural America as a child had many similarities to everyday life in the jungle of Nigeria. I came to the realization that God had been preparing me for his call upon my life even at a young age. I was about ten when my father moved the family from a township in Southern California to a very "back in the sticks" farm in Oklahoma. My brothers and I loved it! We were surrounded by miles and miles of forest and farm land, as well as a multitude of assorted wild animals and beautiful birds. We had plenty of time

to explore and play after we finished our chores and responsibilities. Farm families in those days had no modern conveniences. . . everything was done the old fashioned way. We were living like pioneers. The kids had daily chores and learned how to work. It was that or go hungry. Thank God for this time in my life! It made my introduction to jungle life less of a culture shock than it would be for most people.

The roads, for one, were rutted and unimproved just as I was seeing they were here in the jungle. As a child, the road to the farming area had deep ruts worn in it by horse drawn wagons that were used to carry firewood, hay, and assorted crops fresh from harvest. Some sections of road had deep sand beds and other parts were red clay hills. In the summer, the dry sand swallowed the car up to the running boards if it wasn't crossed with great speed. Yes, we had running boards when I was a kid. And, yes, the kids loved going at a fast speed. But, extracting the car if it got stuck was a tedious endeavor that required digging and finding branches to throw in front of the tires to form a firm footing. The red clay hills during the rainy season became as slick as a slip and slide. If you weren't careful the car could slide off into a ditch that ran alongside the road. I would realize that this was just like the roads in the remote areas of Africa!

Primitive roads require great driving skills. Like my dad, most of the public transport drivers that take passengers into the depths of the jungle or rural areas of Africa have mastered these skills. Their skills have been fine tuned and developed by the necessity needed to successfully manage their many road trips and emergencies.

Resourcefulness required

The lack of funds available in contrast to the prevailing need makes resourcefulness absolutely necessary no matter which continent you call home. I have seen great creativity, not only in my dad and other farmers who solved problems without capital, but also in the African people in all the nations in which I have ministered.

Even the children seemed to have this ability to be creative and resourceful. I was especially shocked to see the children playing with what looked like a soccer ball. I joined them out of curiosity. Upon close examination, I became extremely impressed. The children had used pieces of trash and random pieces of string to create their own makeshift soccer ball. I would have liked to have kept it to show children in America. These children who had little to nothing were able to create a realistic looking soccer ball from trash they found laying around. What creativity and talent!

The people of rural Africa have found ways to make it possible for a vehicle to get into the bush. They, too, are inventive in their solutions to make the impossible possible to drive through. Public transport, and I don't mean buses, can't come to them without a thoroughfare. I have seen many examples over the years. This, being my first mission trip, left me speechless. There was even a road that veered around an old tree that was very large and obviously was not going to be removed. I truly got to see God's gift of creativity at work in the lives of ordinary people.

Old fashioned way

The lives of the rural people in Africa are by no means easy. There are no modern conveniences at all. I did not see so much as a bicycle in this area of Nigeria. Your feet are depended on to travel and a person's head is depended on to carry the supplies or load. My childhood experiences sure helped with this lack of amenities, and that was a good thing! Here in Nara, we not only lived among the villagers, we lived as they lived. The hardest thing for me to handle was the lack of electricity because of the heat and the total darkness at night. Remember, I had asked for a fan. There had been no electricity on the farm I lived on growing up, but I had been a kid. Also, the lighting had been compensated for by lamps/lanterns. So this was a change, but not as drastic as it would seem to other travelers from America who had not had the childhood experiences that I had.

A jungle hike

One day, Chenurea and I had a mission when we went for a walk. This was in response to a night dream/vision that I had and then told her about. In the vision, I saw a huge idol sitting in the corner of my room. This was my first mission trip and I was unfamiliar with the gods and beliefs of the people. I asked Chenurea if idols were kept in the corners of the villager's houses. That is if you deemed a round house to have "corners". She told me that they did keep idols/gods in the house. She also told me that if I wanted to see the main god of the village, she would take me to see it. I got my camera and we were on our way. While I don't suggest going to see foreign gods or idols, I was a new missionary and wanted to not only know what I was up against, but how best to reach the people in the village.

The walk was a long one, and our time before the women's evening meeting was short. But in spite of the pressure to get to the village quickly and back again, I enjoyed the walk. I noticed that many of the areas where food stuff was being grown were not in cultivated fields. Pineapples had been planted at the base of many trees as had some vegetables. Okra was growing by the side of the road in a few places, and I'm assuming that someone had planted it. I also saw some patches of cultivation containing cassava plants and ants - big ants. Nigeria has some of the biggest ants in the world! These ants were huge. They may have seemed even bigger to me at the time since they were marching in a wide formation across the road. (They were not in a single file line like I was used to seeing.) They were not creatures with which I wanted to have a close encounter. But, we would have to cross their trail if we were to go see the god of the village. This was indeed the most impressive ant colony that I had ever seen and have ever seen since. I decided that I wanted to see what the village god was like so badly that I was willing to chance crossing the trail. Chenurea was calm and collected because she had been living among the ants all her life, as had the ladies that tilled the cassava patch. I wondered if the nationals were ever bitten by these oversized insects or if they had something that repelled the vile creatures. I also could not fathom why they didn't simply exterminate them. I personally would have given a lot at that moment for a hundred pound bag of ant powder. However, I took my fears in hand as I was so determined to see one of the African gods. My curiosity was at an all time high. What would the thing look like? What was it made of? How did these deceived souls worship it?

I decided to get a running start and try to cross the ant path. If my jump was short, perhaps since I was a running target it would help me escape from being bitten. My thinking had been sound, I emerged on the other side of the trail bite free. I'm sure some of the village ladies had a grin on their faces after watching me.

This is deity?

We arrived in the village center just before dusk. There was a small fenced area in the center of what I presumed was a park in the center of the village. Chenurea pointed to what looked to me like a bundle of rocks tied onto the end of a rope which was hanging from a pole, much like a tetherball would be. She told me that this was the god that we had come to see. She said that the worship of the god included traditional pagan dancing around the pole and then blood was poured around the base of it. The offering is, I hoped, animal blood. I had heard that goat blood is often used. In light of this information, I remembered why Nancy and I had come to this place. These people needed the true and living God. They needed deliverance from bondage to their demonic entrapment. I thanked the Lord for the opportunity to be a part of presenting the gospel message one on one to the people, and for the chance to be a part of helping to equip the pastors and evangelists for their job. These men and women would be the most effective missionaries since they knew the culture and the people. They could endure the hardships of the most remote areas of their nations.

The light of day was rapidly disappearing, so I snapped as many pictures of the god as I could, as fast as I could. I had been holding back on taking pictures because two very old women had been watching us since we had arrived. They had very disapproving expressions on their faces. They looked as if they might come across the road and challenge us. I felt very protective of my small camera, so I put it back in my bag. We started back to the bible school walking as fast as our feet would carry us.

Family chooses demons

Chenurea and I talked as we walked. I had a lot of interest in the things that she could tell me about her family and her culture. I learned that she was not from this area and that her family lived in a village a long distance away. She told me about the religious beliefs of her tribe. She said that mammy water spirits, vicious spirits that live in bodies of water, were the main spirits that her people worshiped. Her parents and all her family were still engaged in the worship of these gods. She was the only one in her family that had been saved. She had a heavy burden for her family to receive Christ. Each time that she went home for a visit, she tried to witness to her mom and the rest of the family members about Jesus's love and the plan of salvation. Finally, after they had become tired of listening, she had been told, "This family worships mammy water, and our ancestors worshiped mammy water. We will continue to do so." I asked Chinurea if her family knew that they were worshiping demonic spirits, and she said that they did know. Traditions are hard to kill!

We arrived back at the school compound just before it became too dark to see. I was feeling blessed. I had crossed the ant trail two times and had not suffered a bite. I had also learned so much about the villagers. But, I still had so much more that I wanted to learn about these beautiful people and how to bring them to the Lord.

Further insight

When Nancy and I arrived in Africa in the city of Lagos, I had watched the news on tv. One of the lead stories concerned the death of several preschool children.

That morning a preschool that is located on the second floor of a building in Lagos had several children that fell to their deaths. The newscaster went on to say that the caretaker saw a woman coming toward the stairs that led up to the school. The teacher claimed that the woman was not actually a woman, but a mammy water spirit that had taken the form of a woman. Knowing the viciousness of these spirits, and that they steal children, the teacher took action. In an attempt to save the children, she tossed them out of the second story window. She was hoping that they would survive the fall. The woman who was suspected of being a mammy water spirit has not been seen since that time.

I have paraphrased, but in no way have I changed the message of the story on the news that day. I have been told in several African nations that these demons do take the form of women at times.

Bible school night visitor

We had been teaching for several weeks at the bible school in the jungle village of Isiobo-Nara. Our schedule had been planned to take advantage of every possible moment. We taught the pastors, evangelists and other church leaders in the school by day. In the evenings, we held women's meetings or crusades. By the time that our long work day was finished, we had only enough energy left to crawl into bed. However, in spite of my exhaustion, many nights I would lay awake unable to fall asleep. I was new to jungle life, in fact, this was not only my first night in the jungle but also my first missionary trip. I was not accustomed to the night noises and the oppressive heat. And I was definitely not at ease. The cook had graciously given her room over to me for the duration of our ministry time in Nara. As grateful as I was, the room had a big deficit… it had a huge hole in one wall where a window should have been! This was a great challenge for me. The hole faced a portion of the jungle that appeared to be uninhabited. The nights are the darkest dark you can imagine. Even if there is a full moon the canopy of the trees block the light. To make matters worse, fear of the unknown can become a problem for me and lead to anxiety. Thoughts and wild imaginations began to run rampant through my mind concerning the hole and the possible array of creatures that might use it as a means to enter my room. The only comfort that I had was remembering that Chenurea would be sleeping in the kitchen supply room on the other side of the door. And, she was fearless!

Due to my utter exhaustion, I finally fell asleep, but I woke up intermittently throughout the night. Each time that I awoke something new attracted my attention. At one point I heard the sound of something scurrying across the floor. I retrieved the flashlight that I kept near my bed and swept its beam around the floor to try to find out who or what the intruder might be. After all, the hole in the wall was window size and a good size animal could easily fit through it. I shuddered when I saw that it was a huge rat that was creeping through the room. But, I was also happy that it was a small game critter and not something of the larger variety! The rat was presumably on the way to the kitchen's storage room which was attached to the cook's room. The next day when I reported the rat to Chenurea, she was irate that the creature had trespassed in her space. She vowed to keep her short handled broom nearby so she could smash the culprit if it dared to make a second attempt into her territory. I just loved her and her determination and fearlessness.

Death and grieving

A few nights after our arrival, one of the villagers died. That night the air was filled with the sound of the wails of the grieving relatives and friends of the deceased. This made sleeping almost impossible for me. I laid on my bed wide awake listening to the eerie vocalizations that seemed so close that it felt as though I could reach out and touch the mourners. I had been told there would be intermittent drumming, moaning and drunken revelry for several days and nights to mark the passing of this unfortunate soul. These sounds were the sounds of pagan funeral rites, again something I was not accustomed to. I believe in this case the body was to be cremated. Earlier in the day I had seen a scaffold in a clearing near the school. The villagers would likely use this to hold the body for it to be burned.

Evening services

The evening meetings were different than anything I had ever encountered. There was extreme opposition from Satan and his accomplices - the individuals in the area that practiced witchcraft in all of its many forms. The disturbances during our teaching time for the women took many forms as well. The ladies talked among themselves and even across the aisles, some women fell asleep, in addition, the children were unruly and babies cried for no apparent reason. We left the meetings each evening feeling completely drained and feeling as beaten up as if we had run into a brick wall. We started thinking, "What's the use?" At this point, God gave us revelation. It became clear that the situation was a ploy of Satan to hold onto his territory. We should have realized this earlier, but being overtired can cloud the obvious and we were on the edge of collapse.

The heat was unbearable. The most frustrating thing for both Nancy and myself, was the fact that the school had a generator. The dean allowed it to be used for only a couple of hours after darkness fell. This was just long enough to have light to get the day's paperwork completed. This also meant that the fan that the cook had graciously borrowed for me was totally useless!

We begged the dean to allow the generator to be used at night so our fans could cool us enough that we could get our much needed sleep. He insisted that we could not do so. We were "dying" from the extreme heat but he was saving the generator or so he said. Welcome to the life of a missionary.

Fasting - a necessity

In spite of our weakened condition physically, we knew that to have success in our efforts to win the village ladies to Christ, spiritual warfare would have to be done. We decided that fasting was the place to begin.

For me, this was not much of a sacrifice other than adding to my already weak body. Most of our meals were prepared by Chenurea who had served as a cook for Nancy a few years before when she had helped start the bible school. I was very happy that we had her to help us, and I found her to be delightful. I was also sure that she was a good cook. But, let's face it, African food made from things gathered in the jungle was a bit of a challenge even for an adventurous eater like myself. For example, the taste of a particular soup that Nancy had learned to like in her years serving reminded me of the smell of dirty socks. Now, please understand, that was just my opinion. It is a popular dish in Nigeria. I am sure that Nigerians would find some of our foods just as distasteful. It depends a lot on what you are accustomed to. Also, in regards to food, were the bugs. Every meal we ate, we were constantly trying to dust the multitudes of bugs off our plates. They were attracted by the kerosene lamps.

We were not very successful. Don't laugh, but this was minor compared to trying to extract bugs from our blouses after they had swan dived into what should have been private territory!

Nancy and I fasted, prayed and took authority over the enemy for three days. I am sure this was not popular with Satan. He is a defeated foe and he knows it, but he had counted on us not realizing he was behind the problems until it was too late. During our days of warfare, the devil took angry notice that he was losing the fight. On the evening of our last women's meeting, just before service, he made a last ditch effort to stop us. He stirred up the juju (voodoo) people to use their occult arts against us. While we were sitting on the floor praying right before the service was to begin, I suddenly had a searing pain between my shoulder blades. It took me by surprise. It was so painful that it was hard not to scream. On inspection of the wound, it was found that I had sustained a serious burn. How it happened sitting on the floor in a room, I don't know. How did a person send a spell to inflict a burn from a distance? Again, I don't know.

I do know that the burn was real and a source of pain during the last weeks of the trip, partly because of location and partly because of perspiration. However, this was a small price to pay for the success that our ministry efforts to the women reaped. The glory of God came down during that last evening meeting. The women weren't distracted and didn't talk. The children were quiet and behaved and the babies didn't cry. When the altar call was given for those to receive Christ and to get prayer for their needs, there was no hesitation. The women rushed forward. It was an awesome thing to see the power of God setting these captives free.! At the end of the service, we asked for testimonies. The women were eager to tell what God had done for them and we were equally eager to hear them. There were testimonies of salvation, healings and deliverance. One woman told us that she was starting to cook dinner when something told her to come to the meeting. So, she stopped everything and obeyed the voice, even though she did not know who had spoken to her. (We knew it was God and that he had wanted her there for a reason.) She received both salvation and healing that night.

The joy of the Lord shown from the faces of many of the women. Their indifference and coldness had been replaced with love, joy, and praise. As we witnessed the awesome changes that the Lord had made in their lives, all thoughts of the difficulties and discomforts of our stay melted away. We were so glad that God had sent us!

Jujumen

The jujumen, witchdoctors and witches do not want the Gospel message to be brought into their territories. They are eager to rid themselves of the intruders. And yet, they relish the opportunity to see if their satanic powers are greater than that of the true God, God Almighty. It is a given fact that the ministers of the Gospel that show up in their area will have juju and witchcraft focused on them every time they minister in a public place. The things that I learned that these occult practitioners could do, were mind boggling to my American mindset. However, in no case did we ever see God fail us! The futile efforts of the unfortunate souls that attempted to overcome God's power, brought many of them to their knees in repentance to accept Christ. This in turn, so impressed the local villagers that they changed sides too. Then a church could be planted in the place that had beforehand been a heathen demonic stronghold.

A friend of mine shared this story of his and his team's encounter with a juju man. There was one man who had been born into a family that had practiced juju and witchcraft for generations. By the time that we met him, he had collected seventy five jujus, each for a different purpose. His demonic powers were so great that he was feared by all the people of his area. Two of the most outstanding powers that he possessed was that he could fly/levetate like a bird, and cast a death spell without ever seeing or even knowing his victim.

We met him as we went house to house to witness. He listened as he was told about the love and the power of God, but he would not believe the message. A few days later we were having a crusade in the nearby village of Pepesu and I was shocked to see him in the crowd. When I gave the altar call, he came forward to receive Christ. He later told me that when he heard that I was having another crusade meeting, he decided to come and try his powers against me. He was surprised to find that his "magic" had no power against me at all. He then realized that God's power IS greater, and he decided to switch sides. (This is a great reason to have a prayer covering.)

His brother and his wife and children were so impressed by the change in this man that they also were saved. The brother had also been a powerful juju man. These salvations were wonderful. But another astounding miracle took place because of this man receiving Christ. His eighty-five year old father was saved. The old man had been a lifelong juju man and was so strong in his demonic powers that he could walk through solid ground, for example a mountain. In every way he was even more powerful than his son. But he also surrendered his life to Christ because of the change he saw in his son and because his son gave up his juju charms to be burnt. The devil's great agents are now on God's side! They are faithful and quite active in the church. They are strongly serving the Lord! Amen, God is good!

7

MINISTRY IN GHANA

When I saw the car that Pastor Victor had arranged for us, I knew we were in trouble. It would be a challenge, if not an impossibility to get all of the luggage into the vehicle's small trunk.

Transportation problem

The car belonged to one of the church elders and the size of the car had not been well thought out in regards to the passengers and luggage. After much rearranging and trying to pack the luggage into the trunk, it became evident that no amount of rearranging of the bags was going to work. There was simply not enough space to contain it. It was finally decided that we should get in the car and the remaining luggage would be packed on and around us. Everything that was "trunk overflow" was piled on us and stuffed under the back seat. We felt wedged in and weighed down. But, we were happy that everything was coming with us and we didn't have to get a second vehicle, which is very hard to come by.

Clown car comedy

The hotel we were to stay at while making final preparations for the crusade was in a rural area. It was too far from the city for us to come back for supplies for the mission and our stay in the bush. This made it mandatory for us to do in-city shopping for necessities before leaving for the hotel. It is not that there are no supplies in the bush, but it is limited. There is a farmer's type market once a month if there are several villages nearby. But the items that are available are unpredictable and in limited supply. In addition to the market, some villagers put up tables alongside the dirt roads. They have candles, matches, kerosene, and bars of soap, but not much more. Occasionally, they have pineapples or bananas. The only other item that I have seen is gasoline. The petrol is sold in glass bottles of varying sizes. This is mostly for the public transportation vehicle known as the 'boneshaker' van. It looks like a stretched Land Rover and can hold up to twelve people comfortably, but they always cram in more. It rarely comes to the remote areas, but since it is the only ride out to civilization, it is in high demand. The moment people see it coming, they run for it. All the rest of the time, their feet are their only transportation. Africans can walk an incredible distance, and they do it with large loads on their heads and in the pitch black dark.

As our shopping stops progressed, it became harder and harder to free my coworker and myself from the pile of purchases that had been added to the original bundles and luggage. Each time we returned to the car, the whole packing scenario had to be done again. Getting in and out was tedious for us, but amusing. The process reminded me of a slapstick comedy routine or a circus clown car.

Less than adequate hotel

Just before nightfall, we reached the hotel where we would be staying until the last details for the trip could be finalized and the supplies and equipment loaded onto a bus. Remember that communication about mission trips was done via "snail" mail. Many details were not finalized until the missionary actually made it there.

I had stayed in run down hotels before, but this one left a lot to be desired. The best part of being in this place was that Victor's wife could cook our meals and have them brought to us. We were near their home and the hotel had no restaurant. Our room was located next to the bar and we would be sharing the toilet with the bar patrons. This was new to me. I had no idea that the bar had an adjoining room. But then, each time I have stayed here, I have learned something new and surprising about this place.

During one stay, Nancy and I had learned that there was a resident prostitute. We became acquainted with her. She told us that her husband had abandoned her and that she had been left with only the clothes on her back. Since she had no funds and no skills, she had accepted the hotel owner's "deal" for room and board in exchange for the earnings that she would bring in. We listened to her story and in time she listened to us as we told her that Jesus loved her and wanted her to accept him. She allowed us to pray with her for salvation. We also prayed that God would give her an honorable means of support.

The hotel was owned by a chief that presided over a fairly large area of Accra. He was the first chief that I had the chance to spend time getting to know. He wore a multitude of rings and chains, as most, if not all chiefs do. The jewelry have either witchcraft or juju spells on them for the protection of the wearer. The chief had a wife or wives, I wasn't sure which, and a son that was in his twenties. His son kept insisting that I should bring him to America. He even got his father to try and pressure me. This was awkward during my stay since the chief was accustomed to getting his way. In this case he would have to learn to take NO as an answer.

Pack up day
The day before we were to travel to Togo, our destination for this year's mission crusade, Victor's young ministers had to assemble and inventory all of the cargo that would be required for the jungle trip. There would be thirty-six of us going, including the four man bus crew. This number included the youth soccer team from Victor's church, the musicians, as many of the women from his church as could go, and those of us on the ministry team. We had to take sound equipment, musical instruments, a generator to supply electricity, wiring and all of the necessities for lighting the crusade venue, bush lamps to illuminate our eating and sleeping areas, flashlights and the very important chamber pots for the two American ladies. It wouldn't do to have us hiking through the jungle at night! Then there were the pots and pans for cooking for all of us, the dishes for serving food, the groceries that we couldn't get in the jungle, water buckets, wash pans, dish pans. There would also be our luggage and other things that I can't think of. Shopping for all these things should have been my job and Victor's job. It became Victor's job due to my late arrival.
Victor's wife and daughter were terribly overworked the day before trips, and during trips. They would have to cook for everyone and also do the dish washing. That is a lot when we would be ministering for one week… day and night. Victor's daughter was also one of the singers on the worship team.

Getting it all together
The meeting place for those of us that were going to Togo on the bus was Victor's church. The time that we were to meet and the bus was to arrive was eight thirty AM. Those of us that don't use African time were there long before the bus and before many of the team members got there. On a positive note, the bus arrived not too long after the designated time and the huge job of packing the cargo into and onto the bus got underway. Somewhere along the packing, the band member that was in charge of equipment discovered that no one had gone to collect the amplifier that had been rented! panic set in as he realized that perhaps the amplifier had been rented out to someone else when it was not picked up. He headed out to "hopefully" collect it. At ten AM the packing was still in progress, and we were still minus the amplifier and the soccer team members. (It was amazing to me that the area of Togo where we were going even had a boys' soccer team. And, not only that, they had uniforms. A man from Accra that had settled in the village was to thank for this blessing.)

On the road
By eleven AM everyone had arrived, the amplifier collected and packed, and we were ready to go. Every conceivable place that anything could be crammed was filled, both inside and outside the bus. We were finally on our way! The

trip was projected to take eleven hours. This usually meant that it would take fourteen to fifteen hours. More often than not, the delays were due to mechanical problems that the vehicle encountered enroute.

The moment that we started our journey, the kids that made up our music team brought out drums and tambourines and started to play and sing. They were excited, this being their first mission trip. Victor encouraged them to drum and sing loudly. He had placed a sign advertising the crusade on the side of the bus and the singing would attract attention. He hoped the travelers from the area would be on their way home and attend the crusade.

We didn't get far until we discovered that the vehicle's shocks were less than sufficient. To make matters worse, the bus was seriously overloaded. It rocked and swayed like a ship in a storm! The swaying caused the five gallon buckets of water to slosh out on all sides. We had been wondering why the crew had brought so much water. Moments later, the radiator boiled over and spewed water onto the windshield! The driver pulled over to the side of the road and the crew members closest to the door took a bucket of water and refilled the radiator. This process was repeated three more times before we even got out of Accra. The buckets were refilled at nearby houses. Just to comment on the condition of the bus, a bus owner would be very negligent to allow one of his buses that was new or in good condition to travel over the unimproved jungle roads. Thus the reason for the mechanically challenged vehicle. Another interesting thing happened as we traveled. From time to time, policemen or soldiers that were waiting for transportation flagged us down. The bus that had started out full, kept adding more. Each time an official wanted a ride, a short wooden stool was brought out from somewhere and placed in the center aisle. Soon the center was filled with people as well.

Making up time!

The driver did his best to make up for lost time. He had the bus going as fast as it was capable of moving. Soon we reached a mountainous part of the road that had many sharp curves. But, the driver did not adjust his speed. The turns, when taken at a high speed, caused a surprising thing to happen. On every curve, that was to the right, the passenger door swung open. It would not stay closed! Several times we almost lost the youngest bus crew member since he was the one sitting next to the door. The remedy that was settled on to keep him in the bus, was for the man sitting next to him to put his arm around him and grip his shoulder. This dangerous seat is the very seat that I had tried to have assigned to me before the trip started. My thinking was that I would not be so jammed up in that seat so my back wouldn't hurt the whole trip. Every time I sat on it as the preparations were being finalized, one of the bus crew would shout something to me in his language and shake his head no. I now understood. He had been trying to save my life. I might have been a bit annoyed at the time, but thankfully God was looking out for me!

Leaving Ghana wasn't easy

We finally reached the Togo/Ghana border in the late afternoon. We had to stop and check out of Ghana and into Togo. This turned out to be the most shocking situation that we had faced thus far. Victor, in all his busyness, had not remembered to check the bus driver's paperwork. The man had not gotten any of the documents that were needed to take the vehicle out of Ghana or into Togo. Victor, who was well known and loved by the guards at both borders, tried his best to get them to issue permits or to just let us cross. He failed miserably. The only concession that he could get the Togo guards to make was to let the bus be brought across into Togo and to be parked at their border station. This would leave us without any way to get the people and the cargo the long distance that we had to travel to reach our destination. There is no transportation in the bush, as mentioned earlier, and we had reached a remote area. The guards are not like in America when you go between states. These men are fully decked out in military garb, each brandishing multiple guns, one of which was a semiautomatic rifle. They were not the kind of people you "messed" with.

Victor and the driver went into a huddle to discuss what to do. They finally came to an agreement and had everyone reboard the bus. Much to our surprise, the driver and Victor's plan was to make a run for it! The driver put the gas pedal to the floor. This did not make such a desperate move safe by any means. The guards from both border stations were waving and shouting, but we were blessed because they were not shooting. Thank God! I ministered in one nation for many years where the guards would definitely have been shooting.

Dangerous roads

We reached the end of the pavement shortly after entering Togo. The road was now dirt and heavily traveled. Everytime a vehicle passed us, there was a fog of powdery dust that sifted in around the door that would not stay shut and in the sides of the windows. The dust made it difficult to breathe, and to make matters worse, the visibility on the road became zero after a car or truck passed. One of the boys on the soccer team mentioned that he had a brother that lived in the village where we were headed. He said there was a shortcut that would get us off the more heavily traveled road. We should be coming to it shortly. Victor was worried because it looked like darkness would fall before we reached the turn off onto the unimproved road/shortcut. We did reach the turn off while there was still some light. This was a good thing as I don't think we would have found these two ruts through tall grass, weeds and trees "road" in the dark. In my opinion, it didn't really qualify as a road. By this time the sun was setting quickly and darkness was taking over.

Then we learned about the most frightening shortcoming of the bus that I am sure the crew already knew about. In any case, every time the bus hit a bump, the headlights went off for a minute or so. On a normal American road, that might not have been so bad. But we were on a very bumpy and vegetation covered shortcut, and the driver was navigating it in the pitch black dark much of the time! We went along like this for quite a while, the road being further than either the driver or the soccer player remembered. Suddenly the wheels on the left side of the bus fell into a very deep hole. It tipped over to the left side, but not quite all the way to the ground. It did feel like it was being pulled that way by the heavy load of equipment that was packed on top of the bus. At this point, the Holy Spirit prompted me to shout, "Get off the bus!" Everyone got off immediately. We had all stayed on board to this point because we had no idea what the condition of the ground was. It was quite dark and we couldn't see anything and we didn't have flashlights handy.

As soon as we got off the bus we heard people talking and they seemed to be getting closer. Shortly, two men from the village where we were headed arrived. They told the driver and Victor that the village was very near and we could easily walk there. They also suggested that the loads be left on the bus until morning. Then men from the village could help unload it and carry the things to the ministry venue. They could also help to right the bus. The walk was a short but challenging one, due to the lack of flashlights. By this time it was well after midnight. It had been quite a trip, but we had arrived safe and sound. But, what would happen when we returned to the Togo/Ghana border? Who knew what to expect from the deceived border guards!

Exhausted, locked out, and settling in
Nancy and I had the blessing of being given the use of a small unfinished house. Upon arrival, we discovered that no one had remembered to get the keys. This meant that we were locked out of our rooms. It also meant that no one had been able to go in and get them ready for use: there would be no pillows, bed linens, window coverings, and water pitchers. Victor, knowing about my breathing issues, had gotten me the room that had two large windows for ventilation.

After a great deal of discussion on the "how to" to get into the locked house, there was still no solution. Time wore on and we stood waiting as there was no place to sit. At one point the Chief of the area had come to see for himself what the problem was. As time passed, a crowd of villagers began to grow, curious to see the visitors. Getting into the locked building was a lengthy process. I was both relieved and fatigued. But I was definitely too tired to be curious as to how they had gotten into the rooms without keys. No explanation was given, so it remained a mystery, but I suspect someone picked the lock.

It had been wisely decided, during the time the doors were locked, that someone should search for sheets and pillows for our beds. The effort had been met with some success. I was given only one sheet. At this point I didn't care. I gratefully received it and as tactfully as possible made every effort to expel the greeters from my room. As soon as they had gone, I readied myself for bed. The luggage had not been unloaded from the vehicle, so I did the only thing I could think to do short of sleeping in my clothes. I undressed down to my half slip, and pulled it up under my arms and got into bed. I then covered myself with the sheet to partially be shielded from mosquitoes. I fell asleep almost instantly as it was about two AM. There was no point in trying to look at my room. Today had already been filled with enough concerns of its own!

I slept soundly for about three and half hours. I awoke to the sound of loud voices. It sounded like a crowd of people cheering and it was directly behind our house. I lay in bed listening. It was still very dark. Suddenly I remembered, the Africans have early morning prayer before starting their chores for the day. I tried my best to rally enough energy to go, but my body would not cooperate. We would be having two services the first day and one at night, and then every day and night for a week. So I stayed in bed and prayed/slept.

We would be needing God's protection. We prayed for his power to move mightily. We also had a great burden for the lost and deceived souls that lived in this area. This region of Togo had not been "invaded" before this time by people bringing the message of salvation. This would not be popular with the witchdoctors, jujumen, and other Satan serving people. This was a place where the hearts of the people were hardened, rock hard. They had worshiped idols and had been involved in the occult practices all their lives.

Window curiosity

I must have fallen back to sleep, because I was suddenly aroused from my slumber by a noise that I didn't recognize. I did not open my eyes, but I could tell the sun was shining into my room. I realized where I was, and then I remembered that my room had two uncovered windows, one of which faced the road straight on. I then again heard the sound that had initially awakened me, and I realized it was the sound of laughter. At this point my curiosity got the better of me and I opened my eyes just a sliver. I discovered that both of my windows were absolutely filled with faces, and that everyone was staring with delight at the white lady on her bed. I immediately closed my eyes again, hoping they would think I was still asleep. I was thankful that I had the presence of mind not to raise my head to check the noise. Now I was fully awake and alert and recalled that I was scantily clad... and definitely not "fit" for company. Thank Jesus I had put the sheet over me and just on the bed. I'm sure this was a God inspired decision. I clutched the sheet closely around me pretending to sleep. All things considered, I was stuck on the bed until the villagers tired of their gawking and continued to the river to get water, which is where they had been headed. The river was the only source of water in this place, and the early morning chores would make a water supply mandatory. I hoped their morning responsibilities would cause these curious souls to move along. I could not withstand a lengthy wait, nature was calling if you know what I mean. A visit to the outhouse would soon be necessary. Thirty minutes passed and nobody left their post by the window. I was getting desperate and needed to be rescued. My rescue came in the person of Pastor Victor. After seeing my dilemma, he scolded the villagers for their invasion of my privacy and sent them on their way. (By the way, duct tape makes a great window covering!) On a good note, the fact that the people were so fascinated that a white person was in their village was a good sign. It meant that no white people had been in this area before. The crusade attendance would be large, if for no other reason than to catch a glimpse of the white lady. This meant that Victor would have a chance to share the good news of salvation with them.

Getting things in order

Victor's daughter brought us breakfast about 7:00 am, and unloading the bus and setting up the venue was well underway. Our first priority was to go and meet the chief. This was a formality, since Victor had already secured permission for the crusade. When we arrived at the compound we found everything was in place for our audience with him. Chairs and stools from various huts had been borrowed for our comfort. This also was to accommodate the requirement that no one in conference with a chief should be looking down at him, and he would be sitting. After we sat down, the Chief and his linguist joined us. The job of the linguist is that he will be addressed by the person or people that are having an audience with the chief. He will then communicate the dialogue to the chief who gives his answer or input to the linguist to deliver back to the person concerned. Protocol dictated that we were not to speak directly to the chief during this formal time. No one explained the reasoning behind this, but the use of a middle man was the usual procedure. I think this method may be used in case the chief does not fluently speak or understand the language of the guest. He would save face. But, it could also simply be a sign of respect. There are several customs that visitors must learn and observe when interacting with a chief. One other rule which comes to mind is that women must not cross their legs as they sit in the presence of the chief. In fact, crossing one's legs isn't done in the African societies that I have encountered. This is a hard habit for an American to break!

Surprise, surprise

When we arrived at the brush arbor venue, we were happily surprised to see that the publicity had worked in attracting people. The crowd numbered between one hundred and one hundred and fifty people. This was good for a work day. Many of the women in the area would be tending their farms, gathering food for dinner, collecting firewood, washing clothes and doing other household tasks. The men would be hunting and doing… whatever the village men do. I don't know what that is. As I see it, the women do most of the work and that includes the above jobs as well as cultivating the land by hand with short handled hoes.

We also attracted another group of people, the witchdoctors, witches, and jujumen that were for hire were there in force. They had done something that was almost unbelievable. They had gathered together in seven different teams and spread themselves in groups all around the venue. Even Victor had never seen this done before and his father was a juju man. The men and women that practice the satanic arts are fiercely competitive. Yet, they had joined forces and divided up into teams. They had not come to try their powers, they had come to kill us with their powers or try to do so. They would stick together as long as we were in their area. After we were either dead or gone, they would again be pitted against each other to gain dominance of the region.

The pastors had done a good job in venue choice. But there was still a need for vigilance. The devil's number one goal was to try to kill the ministers. But, if that failed, he would settle for being able to kill someone… any one. He didn't care who died so long as the crusade was destroyed. A death would stop the crusade, because the people for the most part would scatter. Many of the locals would become involved in the three-day death funeral practices. We would not be able to minister, nor be effective. A death during a crusade happened perhaps two times during our years of pioneer evangelism. The unsaved villagers flock to the pagan funeral. There are three days and nights of drinking, eating, dancing, and revelry - all costs are paid by the family of the deceased!

Praise time

Africans love to dance. And truth be told, I love watching them dance. Dancing is a part of who they are. The Ghana people brought their beautiful and graceful dancing style into their praise and worship time. Each dance in Ghana and Togo tells a story. More than likely, the dances tell a story in all African nations. One of my favorite Ghana dances means, "Satan is under my feet". At one point in the dance, they stomp and wipe their feet, envisioning Satan being crushed beneath them because of Jesus. The people love to dance so much that after the night services the band and singers are not finished. They play and sing until the early morning hours. The heathens often come and dance too. I didn't always know what story their dance was telling, but I trust that any traditional dances that are inappropriate or blasphemous are weeded out by the young ministers. Sometimes, these unsaved dancers learn one of the praise team's dances. Since the message of the dance always points to Jesus, they learn about him in a way that will stick in their minds.

To round out our soul-winning crusade "package" we brought with us Victor's young pastors. He had led these men to Christ, trained them for ministry, and then he had stationed them in his Volta churches to shepherd the sheep. These men served as interpreters, prayer warriors, and ministry team members who prayed for those wishing counsel. These ministers of God filled their positions with excellence. The fruit of their assignments was advantageous to the crusade but there is a lot of good that can be said for youthful enthusiasm for life particularly when it includes a zeal for the Lord.

Concerning crusades

Church members from the Volta churches and the Togo churches that were near enough in location to the crusade site, attended the Volta crusades each year if at all possible. They arrived filled with excitement and joy and this was in spite of their journeys. They came expecting God to do great things. They were happy to see their friends from the sorted churches that they had not seen for many months. A few of the people that had been saved, healed or delivered, attended the crusade each year to report to the congregation, to Victor, or to myself, that they were still going on with God and walking in the miracle that he had given them in years past.

God was truly good to me when He called me to minister to the people in remote areas. I loved being in the brush arbor meetings and I was totally blessed to see the enthusiasm with which these "glad to be saved" saints praised the Lord with their whole beings. The church members from Togo were particularly cherished by me. I could learn a lot about perseverance and dedication from them. The Togo saints went the extra mile to be in the crusades. Many of them had risked life and limb as they waded across the swiftly running river that partially bordered both Ghana and Togo in the Volta. And they crossed carrying everything on their heads that they needed for the week of the crusades! These determined people did what they had to do to get there. They did not allow the fact that they had no funds for an entrance visa to Ghana or money for public transportation to stop them. Many of them had walked from their homes to the river on the Togo side, some of them great distances. Then they had braved the swift current of the waist high water, and finally had walked the remainder of the way to the crusade venue. Contrast this with the fact that many of us here in the USA let something as small as a rainstorm keep us away from church.

An elderly man that came to share told about God healing him from an advanced case of TB a few years back. He said he was still strong and healthy. Next a girl that Victor had prayed for to be healed. Her legs had been partially paralyzed since birth. She had been dragging herself along with a stick that she used for a crutch, and she often lost her balance and fell. When we first prayed for her, God touched her. She was so grateful for what he had done and for what he was still doing that she continued to come to the crusades over the years to give an update. She was doing better and getting stronger all the time. Although she hadn't been instantly healed, she came to every crusade to report about her progress and God's faithfulness. She had such faith in God. Her balance was improving and she was no longer falling.

The messages at the crusade were very anointed and had the attention of the people, some of it was good and some of it was attention from those that had come to disrupt the service. The villagers had seen the demonic power of Satan moving in their village. So it was important that they now see that God's power was greater. This was no problem - God is faithful. We had miracles and healings take place regularly. This is what happens when you believe God without reservation!

We could always expect the Spirit of God to move in every service, doing miracles and saving souls. God inhabits the praises of his people. But, by no means am I telling you that multitudes of people were saved every time. True, people were saved, but not great numbers of them, especially if it was our first time in that region. In the most pagan place where we ever ministered, I became discouraged. The Lord spoke to me saying that when ministering in these places that have been steeped in the demonic for so long, the best that can be done is to make a chip in the rock hard hearts of the people. But, when chip after chip has been made in the solid rock, it will weaken and crumble. When we are weak then God is our strength! Return ministry trips must be made, and made again, and again to see these hard places crumble. We might not be the one who sees it fall, but every chip is crucial to God' plan for revival to come.

8

FLY, FLY ALONE

Nancy had gone to Cameroon a couple of weeks ahead of me so that she could find a house that was suitable for a mission house. She also needed to get the mission details in place before I arrived. We would be ministering in the jungle area of Mamfe village and in the surrounding areas. We were also invited to attend Papa Billy Lubanza's "Flaming Fire of God" ministers and church leaders conference in Limbe. I was excited about the ministry opportunities and also because of the privilege of being included in the fire conference. I had attended the conference the year before and I had been tremendously blessed. I had also learned a lot from the very anointed ministers that had come from several nations to teach in the various sessions. Nevertheless, in spite of my excitement, I was feeling apprehensive about traveling alone for two days and nights… and about managing to get through three major airports on my own.

The flight out of Phoenix would be no challenge, but my next stop would be in LA. Getting from the domestic terminal to the international terminal had to be done alone while pushing a luggage cart containing my two large bags and hand luggage, and this was not a short strip. It took about twenty minutes to make the terminal change, and the walk was a bit uphill in spots. The biggest problem was my tiredness from all the effort that had to be exerted to locate and secure the supplies that I needed to take with me, packing my bags and doing the last minute details for the mission here at home. I was hoping I could get some sleep during the ten hour flight to Amsterdam.

Dears and delays

The wait for my evening KLM flight was a long one. I was happy to have the company of a girl from Mexico. I had never been to the area in Mexico where she lived, so she told me many things about what it was like. We had lunch together and just chatted until boarding time. After we had gone through security, we headed for our boarding gate. She was such a dear! Since it was a long walk, she had me put my hand luggage on her cart. Thank God! It would

52

have been a struggle for me to carry the bags so far. I had not thought to bring my own cart. This gal was a great blessing to me in many ways. I believe that God had orchestrated our meeting.

The boarding went without incident, or so we thought at the time. But, once we got seated on the plane, it sat at the gate… and we sat, and sat. We sat for a long time not knowing why we had not taken off. The doors had not been closed, and we were not given any reason for the delay for about an hour. It was finally announced that the delay was due to the fact that a man that was booked on this flight had his hand luggage refused by customs. Since no solution was found, his two checked bags had to be located and returned to him. And so we sat while the baggage handlers, who must have felt overwhelmed, embarked upon the task of finding his bags amongst all that luggage. The task was finally completed in due time, and the captain announced for us to buckle up and prepare for takeoff.

The plane landed in Amsterdam at mid morning and my flight to Paris was not until later that night. Consequently, I had several hours that I could rest if I could get a day room in the airport's lower level facility. I had not succeeded in getting through to the hotel from home to make a reservation, so I prayed for a miracle. After much persistence, I was given a room for the afternoon. God had made a way where there was no way! Hallelujah!

The airport maze

I had to go to Paris to get my connecting flight to Cameroon. When boarding time arrived and I saw the plane that I was to take to Paris, I was shocked and became a bit anxious. It was a commuter plane that held about 29-30 people. This would be the smallest plane that I had ever flown on. I had come a long way from when I was terrified to fly. I had take my first flight on my first trip to Africa to do mission work. However, the size of this plane was still a challenge to my faith. "Okay God, let's go."

I was grateful for the English speaking French lady that sat by me during the flight. Having her talk with me helped keep my mind off the smallness of the plane. Before we reached Paris, I told her that I had never been in the airport where we would be landing. I also told her about my failure to be able to learn an appreciable amount of French. She said she would point out to me the correct corridor to take to the transit area. God was taking care of me again and I didn't even realize it at the time. I had no idea how much help the lady was until I saw the airport. The place where we came into the terminal looked like a maze of "rounded top" halls that ran in several directions. There were no signs at all, not that I could have read them anyway. There were just solid white halls, both ceilings and walls were white. I was relieved when I arrived where there were people. There had been only a few of us that got off the plane and the other passengers had disappeared immediately, leaving me alone.

I arrived at the transit area without incident and had another long wait until time to board the Air France flight to Douala, Cameroon. The hours passed, and near the time for boarding, I realized that I needed to arrive in Cameroon with a bottle of drinking water. I had no idea if I could get drinking water at the Douala airport. I still had a long car trip to get to the mission house. And, it is absolutely necessary for me to have an adequate water supply. It seemed wise to me that I purchase a large bottle of water here. I decided to go to the concession stand and buy the water to take with me. I was grateful the man spoke English. I asked for bottled water and how much it would cost. I am not sure what prompted him to give me such a ridiculous price, but with what appeared to be hostility, he answered, "Eighteen dollars." I had done nothing to provoke this attitude. Why was he so irritated that I wanted to buy water? I certainly didn't understand it. Maybe he was irritated because he thought I wanted to drink bottled water in Paris because I felt Paris water was not safe. That is a guess. I paid the man eighteen dollars due to my great physical need for a sufficient water supply. (That is the most expensive water bottle I have ever bought!)

The trip's last leg
My flight to Douala left Paris on time, and I was glad to be on board the last flight that I would have to take for six weeks. In the last two days, I had waited many hours for flights in four different airports, in three different nations. It was still dark outside so I hoped to get some much needed sleep and settle in under my blanket. However, before sleep could come, the very efficient flight crew began to serve either a very late dinner, or a very early breakfast. Since I had not had food in hours, I took the food but declined the champagne that was being served. However, when I said "No, thank you" to my server, she seemed to be put out. It took me a while to figure out a possible reason for her reaction. (I thought about this instead of sleeping.) I remembered that California also produces wine and champagne, and perhaps she had passengers indicate their preference for American champagne. This is only a possible reason, who knows the real reason for her reaction? She may have had experiences with rude Americans who had "ugly" attitudes. I know I have witnessed a few in my travels and feel embarrassed for America due to their demanding attitudes and complaints.

Arrival
We arrived in Douala right on time. But, I would not know until I reached the baggage claim area if Nancy had made it to the airport on schedule. She had to travel many miles from Buea, where we would be the first week of our mission. Happily, I saw her as soon as I had my luggage collected. I felt excited and a bit surprised that I had made the long, somewhat complicated trip from the USA by myself. But now that I think on it, I was never truly

alone. The Lord had been with me and helped me every mile of the way just as he had promised he would do when he had called me into ministry. This experience has been a milestone in building my confidence. I would be needing confidence in the years to come when Nancy would be taken home to heaven and I would find myself in the position as mission head. *God will take us to some challenging and wonderful places in him, we need only to lay aside our fears and "I can't do it's" and follow him in faith!*

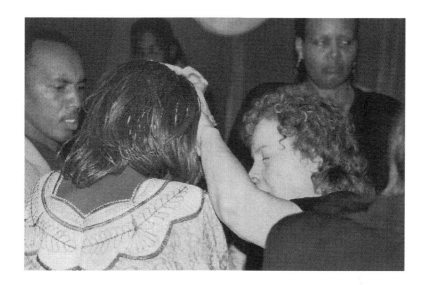

9
KENYA

After ministering in the mission field for some years, I had the pleasure of having my husband, Dock, minister alongside me. He came with me on multiple mission trips to Kenya in eastern Africa. This time, Dock and I had been traveling and ministering daily in small rural villages in western Kenya for more than two weeks. There had been no time for me to do the banking, the laundry, or to finish the preparations for the upcoming minister's seminar. We had reached the point that our shillings were depleted, our clothes were all dirty, and the seminar was in two days.

This last detail was the most serious of all. The seminar was to be held in a mud church in the hard to reach village of Marakusi. The miles of unimproved dirt roads that had to be negotiated to reach it were in far less than good condition. This fact eliminated trying to refresh my memory of the lesson on the way. It would be futile to try to read due to the jostling and bumps. I was the only teacher for the seminar, and the young local pastors, to date, had not had the opportunity to be trained at all. This made the choice of subjects vitally important. Dock and I had been in much prayer concerning this opportunity to sow into their lives. We also prayed for God's leading and guidance.

Laundry and banking
In order to get this project and the other things I mentioned done, the only solution was for me to take a day off. And then pray that one day would be enough time to get it all done. It is hard for an American to grasp that banking and doing laundry can take a long time, but believe me, in Africa, they do.

The laundry was time consuming and back breaking. There are no laundromats. I had to do it in a bathtub by crouching over the tub and rubbing the dirty clothes between my knuckles to dislodge the red mud and dirt. Please realize, I am not complaining, I felt very blessed to have a tub! In rural national type hotels where we most often stayed, I managed with just a bucket of water to wash me, my hair and the clothes. And, it was almost always a battle to get it. Many times, the only water that was available came in a bucket.

Banking takes time in Africa, more time in some nations than in others. In my experience, the process is less involved in east Africa than it is in west Africa. However, it can still take an extended period of time, particularly if a small town bank must be used and the exchange rates have not yet been received from the bank's main branch. Again, east Africa has an advantage over the west African rural banks. Phone communication is more available - more, not always. In any case, my day would be more than filled with the three projects.

Kipkarin

Since I was to stay behind, Dock needed to go with the pastors because the leaders of the village were expecting them to come accompanied by an American missionary. The plan was to attract the people to the open air crusade site by having an extended time of music and singing before the ministry began. The goal for the day was to lead enough people to Christ that a church could be planted. This was vital as there was no church in Kipkarin. It was hoped that seeing the Lord's miracle working power in action and hearing the message of God's love for them would draw them to Christ. This was a particularly strategic location for a church, as there were people living here from several different tribes, with Nandi people having the largest representation. I was told that the place had been settled, in great part, by people that had been forced out of their tribal areas by the fighting that had erupted during a national election several years back.

Election years can become brutal in African nations. Dock and I have been in Kenya during several election years and witnessed the violence first hand. We also witnessed the results of the upheaval. The Rift Valley, during one of those times of political turmoil, had been filled with an enormous refugee camp consisting of tents and makeshift shelters. A vast amount of the displaced people were the widows and orphans of heads of families that had been killed. There were also multitudes of people who lost everything when their homes and possessions had been burned. In addition to having lost so much, many had also lost their jobs (if they were lucky enough to have one)because their places of employment had been destroyed.

A surprise for Dock

Dock had already shown great determination and self sacrifice in continuing to travel over the extremely rough and sometimes almost impassable roads. He had not missed a day of going with us in spite of a very painful back injury he suffered as soon as we arrived at the airport in Nairobi. The injury occurred because all our bags arrived on the conveyor belt at the same time. He did not want to cause a further delay due to having to wait for the bags to come around again. So, he grabbed the first bag and swiftly swung it around to the floor so he could grab the next one, and so on. The bag, being very heavy, brought his spine around too far. We heard a loud snapping sound and he hit the floor unconscious. We knew that his injury was severe, but we did not know how serious because he refused to go to a doctor. He also would not sacrifice the mission.

He agreed to go with the pastors so I could take care of our personal business. When they arrived at the outdoor venue, the meeting place had already been set up. A few chairs had been borrowed from nearby homes for Dock and the two pastors. A man with an electric guitar was there with a small sound system that was powered by a car battery. If a musical instrument is available, which is very seldom, a car battery powers the equipment. This makeshift power source makes a lot of squeaking and squawking sounds. (This is normal to the rural African people. During one trip, I asked the interpreter if we could move further away to see if some of the squawking sound might be eliminated. The young man informed me that those sounds were supposed to be there!) To them, the squeaking and squawking is normal. They are happy with it, and rightly so. To have a musical instrument and a PA system is a great blessing. These things are luxuries that are seldom available.

The music and singing had not been going on for very long before a crowd started to assemble. Between two and three hundred people came to listen, including about fifty children. After the music portion of the service was over, the pastor in charge got up and introduced Dock as the speaker. Surprise! This was a surprise even to him. No one had informed him that he would be presenting the message. Dock wore many hats on the mission field, but preaching, up until now, had not been one of them. Often, having a white person in the places where there has seldom, if ever, been one, is enough to draw a crowd. Thus, Dock had thought that he would just be showing up and being there while one of the ministers did the preaching. But, God sometimes has other plans! Here he was, the featured speaker. He had to hear from God quickly. He decided to go with a simple salvation message. This was fitting, as many of these people knew nothing about the Lord.

No training, no problem

God doesn't only call the qualified, he qualifies the called. Dock spoke about the love of God and his desire to have a relationship with people. Dock loves children and children love him, so he made a point to take time in his message to speak directly to them. The first thing that was done after the sermon was to have a time of prayer for the needs of the people. God's goodness and power were demonstrated as always. Then the invitation to receive Jesus was given. The results were wonderful with between fifty and sixty people responding, including many of the children. A church was established in Kipkarin and the message of Jesus's love will also be taken into the tribal areas. When the new converts return home, the message will go with them. That's the amazing thing with God's kingdom. He may use you to share his salvation message with one person, but the multiplication factor in his kingdom is impressive. That one convert may go on to save a hundred more souls. Never underestimate how God may use you.

God does miracles anywhere
I love the fact that within the anointing that God has blessed me with, is a call to minister in unusual venues. Dock once described it this way, "Ruth is called to a cow pasture ministry, when she stops in the pasture to talk with the shepherds, people begin to come to hear what is being said." This made me happy. Nothing could be better than having the opportunity to tell people that have never heard about Jesus, the plan of salvation and about God's love for them.

One of my favorite venues in Kenya was the place where we ministered on particular occasions near the small town of Turbo, Kenya. The venue was a cow pasture a few feet behind the town. The uniqueness was not the fact that we were ministering in a cow pasture, as that was not all that unusual. The thing that set this place apart was the behavior of the cows that were in the pasture, oh yeah, and the rock crushing facility right next door to it.

Dock and I had gone there with Reverand Kigame, a mighty man of God that lived in a village several miles from Turbo. He had been doing evangelism in the hardest of hard places in western Kenya for many years. He also trained pastors to shepherd the flocks of new christians after he planted a new preaching station where needed. For this particular day of ministry, we had also invited the small youth choir from one of the Nandi Tribe's churches to come and minister in music. Rev. Kigame had started this Nandi church a few years before this time. Also with us was the man who would pastor the new church if enough people gave their lives to Christ to warrant starting one.

We did our setup using borrowed furniture. We had been loaned a small table and two chairs by one of the ladies in town. Our only other equipment was the little portable loudspeaker that I had brought with me from the USA. We had tried to think through the pros and cons of our choice of venue, but we obviously did not consider everything that we should have thought about. The first thing we missed was the cows in this pasture would be moving around as they willed. As it turned out, these particular cows were curious. Their curiosity brought them to the part of the pasture that we were borrowing from them. However, this was a very small hindrance in comparison to the gravel crushing plant that was next door. This detail had not so much as come to mind since it was a weekend when we checked it out and the facility had always appeared to be deserted on Saturday and Sunday. But this was a weekday! Our service had barely started when the crushers were activated to their fullest. The noise that came forth from that facility defies description. And, it started about the same time that I began giving the Gospel teaching. I shouted into the loud speaker as loud as I could. But, I didn't know if anything that I said was being heard since I could hardly hear what I was saying. It would have been funny, if it wasn't so important for the people to hear about the love of God and his saving and healing power. I pushed on, praying that God would make it work for the good of the people and for the cows that were showing so much interest. (It reminds me of Joel 1:20 - Even the wild animals pant for you; the streams have dried up and fire has devoured the wilderness pastures.) We have had cats and dogs that loved to be prayed over, and they even showed reverence as we prayed.

We finished up the ministry by again having the youth choir sing. All of the youth choirs that we have seen in Kenya love to make an entrance. So in keeping with this desire, the kids kept themselves out of sight as best they could in a cow pasture. Then they came marching in singing as loud as they could. It was wonderful, and I am sure that everyone thought so. We gave the call for anyone that wanted prayer to come forward so the pastors, Dock and I could pray for their needs. We were blessed beyond words that in spite of the deafening sounds that the rock crushers had made, some of the people gave their lives to Jesus. It appeared that they had heard the message over the roar coming from next door. There were also several people that testified that God had healed them from their sicknesses.

Miracles

One testimony is of an old and very crippled woman. She had suffered with debilitating arthritis for several years and had been unable to do any work on her small plot of land. We laid hands on her and shouted our prayers for her healing as loud as we could, (because of the rock crushers) hoping that if she could hear what we prayed that her faith would rise. We saw no change at this time, so we committed to her to the Lord to keep working out her healing. Not wanting to leave the woman with arthritis without continued prayer, one of the pastors went to see her the next day. He wanted to see how she was doing and pray some more, but she was not at her house. He asked someone where she was and he was told that she was in her field. The pastor decided to go to the field to see her. He found her there on her knees planting sweet potatoes!

Sometimes healing does not manifest at the moment that we pray. *But, that does not mean that God has not done the work!* The thing to do, whether the healing happens instantly or not, is to praise God for the healing, read the promises of God that tell you about Jesus being the healer, then… watch God move! Whether the healing is instant or a work in progress, healing is promised.

The last person we prayed for that day was the youth choir leader's mom. She had suffered with an almost unbearable ear infection and head problems for months. The doctors had tried everything, but nothing had helped at all. No one knew what had caused the ear infection, but that is beside the point. In any case, when we touched her and prayed for her, God showed up. God came on the scene and poured out his power upon her and healed her. She was so excited that she praised God with such energy and in full health and wellness.

A final word…

There are so many more testimonies I could share. God never ceases to amaze me with his faithfulness to work in the lives of people. God showed up in power on many occasions. He poured out his love and his power. I am so grateful that I chose to say "yes" to his call on my life. I got to see God move in miraculous ways in territories where angels dare to tread!

Now, what about you? Are you willing? Will you ask God where he is leading you and what purpose he has for your life? It may not be the same as mine. There are many ways that God chooses to use his people. There are many places, both at home and throughout the world where God calls people to go and share his goodness. And if fear tries to get a grip on you, don't let it! Step into God's calling and he will be faithful to give his angels charge over you, and in their hands they will bear you up lest you dash your foot against a stone, or injure your back, or get a burn from nowhere, or whatever the enemy may try to throw at you. As a christian, you have authority over the enemy and remember, our God is greater!

ABOUT THE AUTHOR

Ruth Farmer was born July, 1938 and went to meet her Maker, the almighty God in January, 2017. She married Dock in 1954 and they had two sons. She also has 3 grandchildren.
Ruth lived in California, Oklahoma and Arizona. She has served as a missionary in many remote places throughout Africa.
Ruth has left a tremendous legacy behind. There are numerous people that she has trained to serve in the mission field. She has led hundreds of people to the Lord. She has witnessed God moving in mighty miraculous ways throughout her life. She lived a life following the call God had given her.

Made in the USA
Columbia, SC
01 July 2024